Advance Praise for *Authentic Content Marketing*

"There's a new paradigm of content marketing emerging - one based on an ethos of authenticity, caring, compassion, and reaching the clients who you have a soul purpose to serve. George is a brilliant messenger for all of those solopreneurs meant to be making a mighty difference in a world that needs us to step into visibility, reach our tribe, and shine our light brightly."

Terra Christoff, Ph.D.
Soul Purpose Coach for Women
www.TerraChristoff.com

"So many marketing programs simply extract value. They are short campaigns that add no value to customers in any way. George Kao's 'Authentic Content Marketing' presents the exact opposite approach, delivering real value to customers, which create real relationships with customers over time. The concept is simple, straightforward...and the best news is that it works!"

Joe Pulizzi
Founder of *The Content Marketing Institute*; Author of 4 best-selling books about Content Marketing
www.JoePulizzi.com

"George Kao is one of few people out there who have the love and courage to finally challenge the soul-sucking mainstream marketing rules. His work helps heart-centered entrepreneurs to become visible in their unique ways, without betraying their souls and missions. He really walks his talk and is the most real and kind marketing person I know!"

Katharina Zuleger
Visionary & Mentor
www.Aquarian-Leaders.com

"In his new book George Kao teaches us that marketing doesn't need to come with manipulation. In fact, your marketing can really help the forces of good in the world as you deepen relationships and authentically share yourself with others. The end result is a growing business that allows you to focus on your strengths and ultimately helps you to become more sustainable."

Jason Stein
Business Coach for Wellness Providers
www.JasonStein.com

"George Kao simplifies the art of marketing for solopreneurs and small businesses. He has a deep understanding of how to reach out and engage clients in the spirit of caring and generosity. This book, Authentic Content Marketing, is more than a marketing guide -- it's an evolutionary approach to serving in the world with integrity, love and truth."

Fiona Moore
Transformative Mentor and Healer
www.FionaMoore.com

"In his work, and in this book, George provides the solopreneur with a values-based approach to marketing and content creation. He has been a beacon of light and a guide for me since the inception of my site, Love After Kids, and is truly a much needed voice in a world full of hype and empty marketing promises."

David B. Younger, Ph.D
Clinical Psychologist and creator of Love After Kids
www.LoveAfterKids.com

"If you're looking for tips on how to grow your business without compromising your values, this book is for you. George is one of the most authentic business mentors in the world who isn't scared to challenge unethical marketing practices and experiment with new and kinder ways of doing business. Not only is this book packed with practical content marketing tips, you'll be inspired by a compassionate approach to business your customers will love and will help you get the results you're looking for."

Alisoun Mackenzie
The Compassionate Business Mentor, Speaker and Author
www.alisoun.com

"George Kao brings a new and much-needed soul to content marketing, a soul that speaks to the heart. Traditional marketing often manipulates emotion, whereas George's authentic marketing appeals to the emotional self. At the core, George's authentic marketing is courageously based in love."

Stephen Dynako
Author of "The Self Aware Lover"
www.dynako.com

"George boldly paves the way of the future for internet marketing in a way that dissolves fear and fuels love on the planet. A must read for spiritual entrepreneurs who are here to build community and make a difference with their craft."

Claire Shamilla
Energy Healer
www.ClaireShamilla.com

"If you've ever felt 'icky' about marketing and selling yourself and your services, please read this book by one of the best business coaches around. Although 'authentic business' might sound trendy, George will show you how can be true to yourself and generous to others while still using time-tested marketing principles to grow a strong, healthy business that you really LOVE. George Kao is the real deal."

> **Alison Weeks**
> Business Coach and Lifelong Educator

"If you're looking for a truly complete guide to building an authentic and joyful online coaching business then this is the first book you need to read! George has spent years researching, testing and implementing his own authentic business and this book has everything you need to get started. Invest in this book, and give yourself the gift of a business you love!"

> **Andy Burton**
> Author, Speaker & Dream Goal Coach
> www.EagerlyGrowing.com

"Doing something new and different that has the potential to change your life can be scary. I came from the corporate world and I KNEW I didn't want to have a business based on the typical "lizard brain" unethical marketing practices. If I had not found George Kao early on in my process, what I'm creating now would still be a hobby, not a business. With George's help, and the contents of this book, I am learning how create a business based on business savvy -- and infused with soul."

> **Cindy Belz**
> Founder of Footsteps of Wisdom
> www.FootstepsOfWisdom.com

"George Kao broke through his personal limits to create a work based in the higher vibrational values of caring, honesty, and integrity. George has been an inspiration and guide for me, leading the way in proving that goodness and character actually do bring success to business."

> **Keith Logan**
> Sustainable Community Development Consultant
> www.linkedin.com/in/keith-logan-186b46a/

"George is bringing to light an authentic way of approaching business, and a real marketing solution for anyone who wants to create a conversation that is inspiring, uplifting, and engaging. George practices what he preaches, has tested these principles for himself, and is offering a powerful message to those wanting to express in a way that feels true for them, instead of feeling like they must compromise their integrity to be successful. Brilliant."

> **Anastasia Netri**
> Core Genius Coaching
> www.anastasianetri.com

"As the world opens to a new paradigm of authentic marketing and compassionate contribution, George Kao's innovative marketing technology paves the way. With his brilliant soulful guidance I have transformed my marketing platform to create the positive, authentic connection with my clients and audience. With Authentic Content Marketing you will do the same. It provides an eloquent and masterful structure for coaches, small giants and entrepreneurs alike."

    Denise Adele Trudeau Poskas, Ph.D.
    Leadership & Human Strategist Coach
    www.BlueEggLeadership.com

"One of the things that inspires me about George is his enthusiasm for experimenting. George experiments to further develop his philosophy of business, to find what is working in marketing now, and to find new and better ways to market authentically. Over the last few years, George has been conducting experiments around generosity in business, and around developing and delivering powerful content that engages people and builds trust. The results from that exploration are presented here in this book. I highly recommend not only this book, but following George's further explorations and discoveries online."

    Lauchlan Mackinnon, Ph.D.
    www.lauchlanmackinnon.com

"Five pages into George's book, I breathed a sigh of relief. Marketing, as described here by George, can indeed feel authentic, fun and completely in integrity for heart-based professionals. Read this book and apply his principles if you've ever felt that marketing is a horrible way to manipulate people into buying from you. His book challenges that old paradigm and offers practical, actionable tips and mindsets that will change the way you approach your marketing practice. I particularly love his emphasis on 'slow and steady' - if you're an introvert, I believe George's methods could be a game-changer for your business."

    Liesel Teversham
    Confidence and Strengths Coach for Introverts
    www.savvyselfgrowth.com

"George Kao is a rare combination: an experienced and astute marketing professional, and a visionary and compassionate guide to the new paradigm of business. George brings these two ingredients together in his book Authentic Content Marketing. If you've been allergic to content marketing but know it's a key to your success as an entrepreneur, you'll find tons of insightful frameworks and useful tips in this helpful book."

    Maia Duerr
    Author of *Work That Matters: Create a Livelihood that Reflects Your Core Intention*
    www.MaiaDuerr.com

"How do you succeed in business (like, actually) without selling your soul (even a little bit)? George Kao is one of my most trusted colleagues. He constantly tests and experiments and pushes the boundaries of business to figure out how to make more ethical, honest and generous. I love this man's work dearly and refer to him often."

Tad Hargrave
Heart-Based & Sustainable Marketing Expert
www.MarketingforHippies.com

Authentic Content Marketing

Build An Engaged Audience

For Your Personal Brand

Through Integrity & Generosity

By George Kao
Authentic Marketing Coach
www.GeorgeKao.com

This is an unusual Copyright Information page...

I, George Kao, give you permission to copy/paste any part of this book (except for the Foreword which wasn't written by me) and share it anywhere online or offline, as long as you adhere to the license below.

Creative Commons Attribution -- ShareAlike 4.0 International

You are free to:

Share — copy and redistribute any part of this book in any medium or format

Adapt — remix, transform, and build upon the material for any purpose, even commercially.

Under the following terms:

Attribution — You must give appropriate credit, provide a link to the license (see below), and indicate if changes were made. You may do so in any reasonable manner, but not in any way that suggests the licensor endorses you or your use.

ShareAlike — If you remix, transform, or build upon the material, you must distribute your contributions under the same license as the original.

Read more about the license here:
www.CreativeCommons.org/licenses/by-sa/4.0

It's important to me that these ideas get out into the world and implemented, so that more businesses can succeed with marketing that is ethical and generous.
--George Kao

Table of Contents

Foreword by Paul Zelizer, Founder of Awarepreneurs ___ 1

Chapter 1: Four Principles of Authentic Business ___ 5

    1. GENEROSITY with Content. ___ 8

    2. FOCUS on your Strengths. ___ 9

    3. CONNECTIONS with Colleagues. ___ 10

    4. CARE for your Clients. ___ 11

    Reader: I'd love to know something about you. ___ 13

Chapter 2: I had writer's block my whole life... ___ 14

Chapter 3: Three Stages of Content Creation ___ 16

    Stage 1: Casual Content ___ 17

    Stage 2: Improve on What's Liked ___ 18

    Stage 3: Integrate & Productize ___ 19

Chapter 4: Get clear on your "Why" for creating content... ___ 21

Chapter 5: What are the different formats for your content? ___ 25

    Videos ___ 25

    Audio / Podcast episodes ___ 25

    Images ___ 26

    Teleclasses ___ 27

    Webinars ___ 27

    Slideshows ___ 27

    Mindmaps ___ 28

    Articles (or blog posts) ___ 28

    Courses ___ 29

    Social media posts ___ 30

    eBooks ___ 31

    Books ___ 31

Speaking in-person _____ 31

Chapter 6: Which content format is right for you?_____ 33

Chapter 7: What to say in your content?_____ 35

    Method #1. Pause for Ideas after Your Client Sessions _____ 35

    Method #2. Get Interviewed _____ 37

    Method #3. Comment in Groups_____ 38

    Method #4. Summarizing an Article or Book _____ 39

    Method #5. Outdoor Videos_____ 39

    Getting Comfortable with Making Videos _____ 40

    Advanced Method: Interview your Ideal Clients and Gather Tips _ 41

    Advanced Method: Social Media Research _____ 45

    Advanced Method: Keyword Research_____ 46

Chapter 8: How I overcame many years of writer's block _____ 50

    Writing tools _____ 52

Chapter 9: Your Transformational Framework _____ 54

    The Forest_____ 55

    The Trees _____ 56

    The Ecosystem _____ 57

    Steps for Creating Your Transformational Framework _____ 58

    FAQs About Your Framework _____ 59

Chapter 10: Which content should be Free versus Paid? _____ 61

    Keep your free content "white belt" _____ 64

Chapter 11: The Path To Awesome Content _____ 66

    The Two Fantasies of Content Creators _____ 66

    The Ugly Origami_____ 67

    The Parable of the Ceramics Class... _____ 70

    Dangerous: Zero Engagement and Viral Content _____ 73

Chapter 12: Practical Tips for Making Your Content Great _____ 76

    Practice your observation skills_____ 76

What makes your content indispensable? _____ 76

The importance of emotions _____ 78

No more fear-based headlines _____ 79

KISS _____ 80

Don't worry about becoming an Amazon Best Seller _____ 80

Chapter 13: How To Spread Your Content _____ 82

Where does your ideal audience consume content? _____ 83

Sample Email to Your Clients/Friends _____ 83

Which options should you ask about? _____ 85

A simple, effective platform: Your email newsletter _____ 86

Look at the best practices of the platforms you use _____ 90

The Best Distribution is Guesting _____ 91

Make "guesting" one of your key marketing activities _____ 95

Where to look for guest content opportunities? _____ 95

Chapter 14: Keeping Track of Your Best Content _____ 98

Chapter 15: Create a rhythm of content sharing that works for you _ 100

Chapter 16: Even when conditions are not good, I still do my content... _____ 102

Chapter 17: Share from your heart -- and trust the process! _____ 106

You are truly special... _____ 110

Can you help by adding a review? _____ 110

Acknowledgements _____ 112

About The Author _____ 115

Foreword by Paul Zelizer, Founder of Awarepreneurs

"OF COURSE!"

I hadn't even finished reading the email I got from George Kao asking me to write the foreword to this book before I responded back with my answer.

As a former member of the Wisdom 2.0 team, the founder of Awarepreneurs (a global network of conscious entrepreneurs), and a visible leader in the conscious business and social enterprise world, I am connected to many 10,000's of people from around the world in this movement. And I get asked to contribute - in one way or another - to many book projects in this field. Rarely does a project show up that I feel so passionate about.

There are two reasons for this. First, George Kao is an exceptional human being and teacher. Second, I believe that authentic content marketing is one of the single most important topics for anyone who wants to grow a conscious business.

First, let's start with why I think George is the perfect person to write this book.

A few months after George Kao showed up on my radar, he wowed me.

After several years of making a lot of money selling online courses and other leveraged offerings - often in fast paced joint venture alliances - George started publicly talking about feeling he had gotten off track in his business. Even though he was taking a very significant cut in his income to do so, George pulled back from this business model and started solely offering affordable individual coaching.

Once you understand WHY George made this choice, you'll come to understand just why he's become a trusted resource for conscious entrepreneurs and business owners around the world. He is, for instance, one of the most popular marketing teachers for members of the Awarepreneurs community.

George became concerned that many people buying expensive online courses and trainings never made sustainable changes in their business and lives. Learning about this research, he worried whether the people he was selling his own courses to were getting actual results. He wanted to be much clearer about what lasting behavioral change really looked like, when growing a conscious business, and make sure his services were creating real impact.

So George took a radical step - he pushed stop on his very successful business, scaled back, and focused on working one-to-one for two years. He wanted to get a personal look at what real and lasting change looks like.

I would say it worked.

Today, George's practice is full, with a waiting list. He regularly refers people to other conscious marketing coaches. His clients love him dearly, and his name is one of the first to come up when someone asks the Awarepreneurs community about getting help with marketing training. George's clients don't just like and respect him, they are passionate advocates for his work.

Second, let's talk about why I think authentic content is one of the single most important topics for any conscious entrepreneur or business owner.

The foundational practice I teach my marketing clients is that *"Marketing is just Steady Loving Presence in the marketplace."* And one of the very best ways to do this is via a consciously designed and implemented content marketing strategy.

For instance, I currently do a three-days-per-week Facebook Live show called the Conscious Business & Conscious Living show, as well as a weekly Awarepreneurs podcast interview with a conscious business thought leader. As a result, I have a constant flow of new clients for both my individual and group coaching, without ever having to resort to hyped up or manipulative marketing approaches.

George is a master at authentic and value packed content marketing. His blogs, free calls and videos (if you haven't yet seen the videos he makes while he walks his dog Buddy, I highly recommend them) are warm, often funny and always informative. He consistently shares for free what many business and marketing coaches offer only to their paying clients. And thus, George has a waiting list while many of those, with a more stingy approach, struggle to get clients.

In the marketing world, there is a saying "Content is king (or queen)."

In other words, she or he who puts their time and good attention to making high quality information available for their ideal clients, will enjoy a thriving business. In my experience, this is still true - despite the many changes that have occurred in the conscious business and healing sectors.

However, I have one caveat. The content marketing bar has risen. In almost every field, there are people already sharing content freely. That wasn't true decades ago, when many of the currently popular mentor coaches, consultants, healers and practitioners were just getting started.

It's not enough anymore to just put content out there. While it doesn't have to be glitzy, content needs to be highly valuable and well presented. At the same time, if you want people to hire you or buy your products, your content has to give your ideal client the sense that you are a caring, authentic human being.

There is no one I know who better understands both the specific strategies of content marketing, as well as the ways you can build a meaningful and authentic relationship with your ideal client, than George Kao.

So, in this book, you have some of the most important information there is about how to grow a business effectively and ethically. And, it's written by a man who has earned the highest degree of trust from myself and almost every other conscious business leader I know.

George has given the conscious business world a tremendous gift here. I encourage you to treat this book like the treasure that it is. Take your time with the material. Consider going over the relevant sections several times. I know I'll be referring people to it for many years to come.

Paul Zelizer
Founder of Awarepreneurs
www.Awarepreneurs.com and www.FB.com/groups/Awarepreneurs
Wisdom-Based Business & Leadership Coach
www.PaulZelizer.com and www.FB.com/PaulZelizer

Chapter 1: Four Principles of Authentic Business

This is a book about conscious marketing. What sets this book apart from other business/marketing books are the higher values that are foundational here.

Yes, you'll find some excellent, time-tested business tips. Yes, you'll learn how to figure out what content to create, and how to make it more engaging and shared by others... but most of all, you'll discover how the greatest success can come from sharing with your heart.

A lot of people in my audience dread marketing. They view it as a "necessary evil" to get the message out about their passion. Traditional marketing approaches feel icky to them, whether they are receiving that marketing, or being taught to emulate those tactics. Traditional methods do not resonate with their souls.

It doesn't have to be that way.

There is a better alternative.

Did you know that it is possible to create content that is helpful to your business, of genuine contribution to the world, and have the whole process feel enjoyable to you?

This may seem out of reach, but it can be done. My clients and I offer living proof. It starts with understanding what I call Authentic Business.

Here's a story to set the context:

I was listening to an honest conversation between two marketing experts. They were lamenting about how hard it is today to get their content noticed, and what a struggle it is to rise above the noise in a crowded online world, where anyone can become his or her own media channel.

They spoke about how content marketing strategies that worked five years ago no longer work today. Even the strategies that worked well a year ago are no longer effective!

"Things are changing so fast," they said. "We have to hustle to keep up with trends, the latest strategies, the newest platforms."

It was exhausting just listening to them.

The truth is this: Every space online and every industry eventually gets crowded.

Conventional marketing gurus will always try to sell us on the latest strategies by appealing to our fears. They say:

"You don't want to get left behind, do you?"

"You are leaving money on the table!"

"Aren't you afraid of missing out on the newest thing that can take your business to the next level?"

This is the normal way of seeing business -- *Competitive Business* -- and if you aren't paying attention, you may start to believe in it, too...

- *It's a dog-eat-dog world.*
- *Your competitors want to crush you.*
- *You better stay up and keep up!*
- *It's a war out there, people! (Don't believe anyone who tells you otherwise)*
- *It's not going to last forever -- so you better get your share now!*
- *Get the latest and greatest strategies ASAP!*

- *Keep the best ideas a secret, so your competitors don't catch up!*

Are these the values you want to embody, model, and promote in the world?

How can this type of business model be *truly* good for anyone? The *Competitive* Business model is ultimately draining, isolationist, and fear-driven. It is misaligned with our higher values of connectedness.

**

There is a healthier alternative for us.

I call it Authentic Business.

Do what is authentic to your heart, soul, spirit. Do what is aligned with your highest and truest values.

Interestingly, it is also *more effective* for business, but it takes some patience... as all good things do.

Instead of trying to catch up with the latest fad, an authentic business focuses on *truly evergreen strategies* -- ideas that have stood the test of time, and will be around tomorrow, the next decade, and likely into the next century.

The core idea is the *Golden Rule* -- "Do unto others as you'd have them do unto you."

Another way we might say it is: "Use the kind of business strategies that, if more people in your industry used, would create a better world."

By building my business with these principles, I've gratefully earned a comfortable and sustainable income for more than a decade, while living in San Francisco... an expensive city no less!

A popular figure you may have heard of -- Gary Vaynerchuk -- is also a model for this type of business. Gary is incredibly generous with his content, focused on his strengths and values, and models "unscalable" care for his audience. As a by-product of his generosity of spirit and focus, his company's annual revenue is more than $100 million.

Let's dive into the four principles of Authentic Business.

1. GENEROSITY with Content.

Think of content <u>not</u> as "How can I offer teasers to get more sales?"... but rather:

"How can I consistently educate and uplift my ideal audience, while exploring my message and voice? How can I contribute to my industry?"

If you embrace this way of content creation, you will enjoy it a whole lot more!

As a result, you'll become much more consistent in content, and not surprisingly, you'll receive a lot more leads and referrals for your business.

(I found it fascinating that after I became truly consistent and focused in my content, I stopped having to reach out for leads -- they came to me organically, thanks to my content, and filled my coaching practice without my having to work hard at selling.)

Instead of trying to keep the best ideas to ourselves, let's share our best ideas with our clients **and also** our colleagues and our wider audience. That's what Authentic Business is about -- generosity that brings you unbelievable amounts of goodwill and referrals.

Instead of trying to get our little piece of the pie, let's make the pie bigger for everyone.

Can you imagine how the business landscape could look and feel if more business owners thought this way?

Instead of "competitors" I like to think of them as "niche mates" -- other human beings, with unique talents, who want to fulfill their purpose, who want to support their families, who would prefer to be in a collaborative and caring industry. And I hope my "niche mates" will think of me in that way, too.

If you want to see that change in your industry, then be the generous one that leads. You will inspire your colleagues to follow. They will start sharing their best ideas, and you will all progress together, *faster* and *farther*, than you could alone.

With your niche mates, through your collective generosity of content, you will attract more interest in your industry as a whole.

2. FOCUS on your Strengths.

To be authentic means to spend your time doing what you truly love, in your own unique style. If you focus, those activities become your strengths. By focusing on your unique strengths, you fill a gap in the ecosystem of your industry.

This, on the other hand, is not focused:

"My healing modality can solve problems from A-to-Z... for ages from 15 to 85, for all types of people. I am great at helping anyone and everyone!"

This un-focused business has unwittingly become a competitor to all other service providers in her industry.

Another provider may focus on problem X, another one focuses on problem M, but because you say you can **solve A-to-Z**, you are now competing with **all** of them.

The solution? Focus your offerings on your unique strengths.

When you focus on solving specific problems for specific people, you become excellent at your craft more quickly.

This will lead to a deeper sense of fulfillment because you'll see more of the impact you are making on your clients.

Deeply happy clients will then generate much more frequent word-of-mouth referrals for your business. You can then do less marketing, yet have enough clients.

When focused on your unique strengths, you'll also be more successful in creating relevant content.

Don't be in competition with everyone else. Carve out your own niche, serve a specific type of person, do a specific thing for them. Once you've become successful with your focused niche, you can then expand.

To discover your unique strengths to focus on, you will need to experiment. The next principle on connecting with your colleagues will help.

3. CONNECTIONS with Colleagues.

Authentic connections build our network and our ability to make more of a positive impact. No one actually succeeds on their own. Success is built through the support, both direct and indirect, of a community.

Additionally, working with your connections authentically and building your community is fun, and creates the emotional waves of support and joy that make this whole endeavor deeply worthwhile.

Instead of each of us being King/Queen on our tiny, isolated island, let us connect compassionately and authentically with more colleagues in our industry.

As you connect, find out what each colleague is authentically gifted at or experienced with. What type of content are they best at creating? What specific problem do they solve the most effectively and efficiently… and for which type of person? (You are helping them to focus on their unique strength!)

This creates two great outcomes: it helps you more skillfully refer people to them, and it helps you juxtapose your own skills and expertise, so that you can further focus your <u>own</u> unique strengths and help to fill gaps in your industry.

If you and your colleagues compassionately and authentically connect with each other, you can all build more effective services, have enough clients, and create more relevant content.

4. CARE for your Clients.

This is another universal principle that will *always* work in marketing because it has always worked in human relationships. (Ultimately, marketing is about skillfully relating to other people.)

Caring for your clients means that:

(a) You become really curious about who they are, what they love, their fears and dreams, their thoughts, their emotions, how they react to different situations. By doing this, you will naturally create better relationships with them. You'll focus your offerings more skillfully. You'll naturally create content that is more relevant for them.

(b) You care how they feel as they interact with your business. How can you improve the various points of contact that your clients have with you, your staff, your marketing, or your process. How can you improve each "touch point"? Each automated email they get, each time you talk with them, each time they encounter your business -- how can they feel even more delighted or cared for?

(c) Your genuine care for your clients fuels your passion to improve your craft, to be even more effective and efficient at helping your clients.

If you bring the experience of true caring into your business, you'll find that information about your brand will spread organically - and quickly!

**

Unlike conventional business where you hope your competitors don't catch up to the best ideas, in Authentic Business, you actually *want* your niche mates to learn and embody these principles. You want them to apply The Golden Rule as skillfully as they can.

As you implement these four principles deeply into your business, you'll see that marketing will get easier for you.

It is a win-win for you, your clients, your colleagues, and your industry.

To watch the companion video and comment on this introduction, go to this Facebook thread:
www.FB.com/GeorgeKao/posts/10106661722247023

Reader: I'd love to know something about you.

One of the strange things about writing a book, instead of having a conversation, is that I don't know who I'm "talking" to through this book. Can you let me know a bit about you?

If you'd like to help me with this, fill out this short online form: www.GeorgeKao.com/BookSurvey

I personally read every response. After submitting the form, you'll also see some bonus content related to the book.

Thank you!

--George Kao

Chapter 2: I had writer's block my whole life...

Believe it or not, even though I've written a book, I actually had writer's block my entire life... until 2015.

I suffered through 16 years of schooling, then earned a college degree in English literature (where I had to write paper after paper!) Part of the challenge: English is my second language.

Fast forward to 2009 when I started my business -- *in marketing of all fields* -- where writing is of supreme importance. It felt painful every time I had to write an email campaign, update my website copy, or even write a social media post.

For the first five years of my business, I did not blog at all. In fact, I ridiculed the blogging and content industry. I talked (rarely did I get "talker's block") about how bloggers are stupidly giving away so much value for free, when they could be charging for most of it.

Back then, I was selling expensive online courses, and the only thing I was giving away for free was teasers... "free" webinars that were essentially elaborately-designed sales pitches.

Forward to 2014. I had been going through a deep spiritual transformation. I came to see my business practices in a new light -- and I could no longer do it. I stopped selling my expensive ($2,000) online courses, and started providing only one-to-one, individualized coaching, at a reasonable rate.

And I started to give away all my content for free.

I became one of the "dumb" bloggers I was making fun of!

Now I realize: the bloggers had it right all along.

When you create and publish content consistently, you earn enormous benefits over time, provided that you follow the Four Principles of Authentic Business that I outlined in the introduction.

By publishing content consistently, in an authentic and connected way:

- You get smarter, faster.
- You get to see what types of content your audience wants, and therefore what you can develop further, and even monetize.
- You build loyalty with your readers. They see that you care enough to give useful knowledge generously.
- You develop connections with -- and earn respect from -- trustworthy colleagues with whom you can collaborate.
- You build an online presence you can truly be proud of.
- You build a much more sustainable business.

Thankfully, I did eventually overcome 30 years of writer's block, and I will share my methods throughout the book.

Chapter 3: Three Stages of Content Creation

Here's a mistake I see from many wisdom-sharers and aspiring content creators. Maybe you have done this:

You have an idea or framework that inspires you, so you think it must be exciting for other people, too.

You put lots of time (and money) into packaging that idea into a book, a course, or other product, or taking a lot of effort to make an amazing video...

And then what happens after sharing it?

You get nothing.

That idea, framework, teaching, course, article, or video gets little to no response... far less than you expected.

You have fallen for one of the core human biases -- to be inside one's own head about something for too long. You've neglected to test it with enough people to see if that idea, or the way it's expressed, is really something that other people "get."

The sad result: it erodes your self confidence.

Or you may try even harder to share it... and still, you barely get a response. You might then become resentful or cynical.

Worst of all, you might decide to quit your business and go find a secure -- yet passionless -- form of employment.

Always remember this: your passion is not a bad idea... it's <u>how</u> you are sharing the message!

You need to experiment with sharing in different ways, **always in the mindset of testing**, until you discover a way of sharing it that other people easily "get."

The solution is to understand and practice The Three Stages of Content.

Stage 1: Casual Content

This is where it all starts.

For example, I casually make three short videos while on my long Saturday walks with my dog. In each video, I share an idea that I think might be helpful to some clients and audience members.

In fact, what inspired this chapter was one of my casual videos. See the original video here:
www.FB.com/GeorgeKao/posts/10106365973759363

I have low or no expectations about how these casual videos turn out. At this stage, I spend as little effort as possible, so I am less concerned if the content gets any engagement at all.

There's a distinction here: I *care* enough about my audience and my own explorations to keep making Stage 1 Content. Yet I *don't care* how people respond (if they respond at all) because at this stage, it's meant to be exploratory and experimental.

Here are the principles of Stage 1 Content…

(1) Explore a new idea, or try a different way of saying an old idea.

(2) Test the idea with the market by sharing it on social media (or perhaps, at first, with a supportive group of friends), and have zero expectations for responses.

(3) Minimize your energy and time when making Stage 1 Content, since you don't know if your audience will like it at all, no matter how important you believe the message to be. "Casual" is the word that helps me in this situation. Definition of casual: relaxed and unconcerned; temporary or impermanent.

(4) Be prolific and consistent with your Stage 1 Content so that you have lots to explore and test with, spending as little energy as you can for each piece. Remember, you are testing here, not being anywhere near perfect.

Stage 2: Improve on What's Liked

Once a month, go back to your recent Stage 1 Content, and see which pieces received the most engagement (likes, positive comments, shares) from your ideal audience.

Those are the pieces to take into this next stage.

Stage 2 is where you spend a bit more effort:

- Think about how that piece can be improved.
- Would another story/example make it clearer or more interesting?
- Re-write, re-record, and/or re-purpose it into another format (for example, turn an article into a video, or a video into an article.)

Once you've made some improvements, **share the piece again**, but this time with a wider audience. Perhaps you shared your Stage 1 with a small group of friends/colleagues. Your Stage 2 content can then be shared with broader connections and any social media platform you use.

Here's another example of how to re-purpose content: maybe your Stage 1 content was casually posted on social media. Your Stage 2 can be edited and published on your blog. Then you can create a companion *image quote* (explained later in this book) that serves as the blog post's cover image. Finally, you can share the link to the blog post everywhere on social media.

You might also want to personally email the link to more friends/colleagues who might love it, or have connections in their network who would. Let them know that this idea originally had traction, and that you made it even better, and would love to see if they agree. (Always be courteous about how much attention you request from your friends and colleagues.)

Stage 3: Integrate & Productize

Once in awhile, take a look at your collection of Stage 2 content pieces. Chances are very good that some of them can be integrated or combined into one larger piece.

You have the opportunity in this third stage to create something that can add to your legacy and be shared even more widely… perhaps a formal product, such as a book, a video series, or an online course.

In fact, this very book is one of my Stage 3 pieces. It combines some of my Stage 2 posts and videos into a themed and sequenced package, with a nice cover, table of contents, and an index.

**

Your content will have a much greater chance at success if you follow these 3 Stages. Too many people ignore Stages 1 & 2 (or don't even realize they exist), and jump right into writing a book or creating an online course, and are baffled when it's not successful.

I hope this chapter will encourage you to take it step-by-step to try out your ideas and discover what the world actually wants from you, so that you can thoroughly enjoy your content creation process.

"Your calling is where your deep gladness and the world's deep hunger meet."
--Frederick Buechner

Go into Stage 1 with gusto... be casual, be prolific, be experimental, and you will see yourself (and your audience) grow.

To comment on this chapter, and see the Stage 1 video that it originated from, go here:
www.FB.com/GeorgeKao/posts/10106365973759363

Chapter 4: Get clear on your "Why" for creating content...

An authentic business starts with authentic content.

Separate your content from your selling, so that each can be done more effectively.

Yes, you may end up using some content to sell your services/products. However, to maintain the highest authenticity (which serves your business -- and your soul -- in the long-term), focus most of your content on serving, rather than selling.

Let's **first** clarify why content creation is important to you *personally*. There are at least 10 reasons:

1. Create content to clarify your message & your style.

The more you create, the more your message and approach will evolve.

Some people think *"I've got to figure out my niche, my unique message, my offerings, <u>before</u> I can write articles / make videos / etc..."*

The reality is that by sharing your content -- whatever you <u>already</u> know, in whatever voice you already have -- you actually clarify what you're about, who you aspire to be, and what offerings make the most sense.

So <u>start</u> with creating content, in order to clarify your authentic message, uncover your unique genius, and to explore what you might offer in your products / services.

2. Content is a way to organize your knowledge to benefit your clients.

This is especially helpful if you find yourself saying the same thing again, and again, to various clients. Why not write it down, or record it, in a way that can bless many more people?

As your clients receive foundational knowledge through your content, you'll then be able to do even deeper work with them, transforming their lives in greater ways than before.

And those who discover you based on your content, will be more qualified to become great clients for you.

3. Create content to get smarter, faster, in your field.

In the first 5 years of my business, I balked at content creation. I thought it was smarter to hone one single presentation, a webinar, that I could deliver again and again to convert people to become my clients.

Once I got enlightened to the power of content creation, and started creating content prolifically (in 2014), I got so much smarter, faster, in my expertise. I truly wish I started doing this at the beginning of my business.

You'll be amazed when you start creating content consistently. You'll realize that you have an infinitely deep well within you. The more you tap into that well of ideas and content, the more abundance you'll receive.

The more content you create, the more insights will come to you. In other words, creation fuels inspiration.

4. Create content to improve your SEO.

When you create content consistently, the search engines start to take notice, and will start showing your content more consistently.

Those who need your message will start to find you through internet searches!

The key is that this takes time to start occurring. Most search engine optimization (SEO) experts advise that it will take a minimum of 6-12 months of *consistent content creation* before you can expect the search engines to start working for you.

5. Create content to build trust & credibility.

Imagine all the people who could be interested in your work. Imagine having to talk with each of them separately...

That would take way more time than you have.

The solution is to create and share content. You would then reach many potential clients at once. By consuming your content, potential clients can quickly sample your expertise and personality. They will filter themselves out if they're not the right fit. And, the ideal clients will resonate with your message.

Trust builds, as they consume more of your content, especially when they come to see that they can expect *consistent* content from you.

6. Create content to better understand your audience.

The only way to know what part of your overall message is most important to the world is to share it with the world, and then see what gets traction.

Remember *The 3 Stages of Content Creation* that were explored in an earlier chapter.

7. Create content to be top of mind for your audience.

Otherwise, your audience will be consistently seeing *other* people and *other* messages that may be less helpful to them. Your voice is needed!

8. Create content to lead your ideal client to the next step of transformation.

Your content will continue to move your ideal client audience forward in your framework. (see the chapter below on "Transformational Framework.")

By helping them move forward, through your content, they will be more qualified to work with you, because they'll better understand and believe in your ideas and expertise.

9. Creating content consistently is a great way to generously serve the world!

When you create and share content generously, you serve many people, empowering them with the knowledge that helps and inspires them to improve their life / work / relationships.

It is, in my opinion, one of the most leveraged, impactful ways for you to give your time and energy.

10. Creating content helps you discover your calling.

Through your content, you will explore and uncover more and more about what you are meant to do, as you engage your audience, use your voice, and influence the world.

Which of the 10 reasons resonates most with you? Add your comment here:
www.FB.com/GeorgeKaoCommunity/posts/10154738449024867/

Chapter 5: What are the different formats for your content?

Now that you're clear about why it's important to create content, the next step is to choose what format(s) you will experiment with.

All good marketing is about experimentation.

Start with trying one way of creating content. See if it matches your personality and energy. Then try another format and see how it compares.

First, I'll explain some of the different ways you can create content. Then, I'll help you decide which one(s) to choose!

Videos

Nicola Mendelsohn, a VP at Facebook, was quoted as saying that she wouldn't be surprised if most of Facebook's content was "all video" by the year 2020.

And, as broadband internet becomes more widespread and cell phone data speeds increase, Video content will become ever more commonplace.

If you're not already making videos, I recommend that you start doing it casually, as practice. It will take time to get used to seeing & hearing yourself on video! Don't delay that practice. The more you do it, the easier it will get.

Here are some of my videos -- www.GeorgeKao.com/Videos -- which as you can see, are quite casual. I've kept it that way because it works for my minimalistic brand.

Audio / Podcast episodes

I no longer recommend the podcasting strategy to most of my clients, although there are exceptions.

Most people, including me, listen to podcasts when we're not paying close attention. I listen to podcasts when I'm walking my dog, doing the laundry, or in the car. If you as the podcast host then ask me to go sign up for your email newsletter, or register for a webinar, or buy something, I will think "Maybe that's a good idea, but I can't do it right now."

Other methods, such as video or images or text, are where people are paying enough attention that they are much more likely to take a requested action.

Podcasts, however, can be beneficial for these purposes:

- To "give back" to the greater community if you much prefer to create audio content instead of video

- To connect with influencers who enjoy being interviewed via audio, if you are a good interviewer and can help the guest speaker shine

- For brand-building if you're trying to "show up everywhere" for your audience

- To monetize via ads, if you already have a large audience

For years I listened to many podcasts. Recently, though, I've switched over to YouTube Red, which allows me to listen to any YouTube video on my phone, even when the screen is turned off. YouTube, which has the largest collection of free and high-quality talks on the internet, has now become my "podcasting" service. The bonus is that while listening, I can also turn on the video if I want to, and look at the description of the video to go to a link that is being mentioned.

Images

Images have been gaining popularity on social media, and it's only accelerating, with Instagram and SnapChat. If you love taking photos, or creating image quotes, then this medium may be perfect for you.

Here's my post and video about how to create image quotes easily and for free:
www.FB.com/GeorgeKaoCommunity/posts/10154983778499867

Another type of image that can get a lot of shares and traffic are infographics. See samples of recent infographics here:
www.goo.gl/6okeKp

Teleclasses

A *teleclass* is simply a conference call, via phone or VOIP, that can be facilitated using technologies such as www.UberConference.com.

This is ideal for those who aren't comfortable with video, and yet like to teach or share their voice and message.

Webinars

A *webinar* is essentially a live-video where participants can interact with you, like a video version of a teleclass.

On a webinar, you can share slides, or provide access to documents that you can walk participants through during the webinar.

I have created hundreds of webinars since 2009, and it is my favorite way to disseminate content and connect with my audience.

I prefer to call mine "online workshops" because my webinars are more content-rich than many webinars out there, which are unfortunately cleverly-designed sales pitches.

You can register for my online workshops here:
www.GeorgeKao.com/Workshops

Slideshows

Do you like looking at slideshows? How about creating them?

There are several online websites that feature slideshows, and the most popular one is www.slideshare.net. You can find some valuable information there, conveyed in a way that is often more interesting than articles, and more efficient than videos.

As an example, here is my slideshow about niching: www.slideshare.net/georgekao/niching-101-venn-diagram-spirals-artist-entrepreneur-paths

Mindmaps

I love using Mindmaps to keep track of my knowledge.

When I have a new idea that I want to teach in a future workshop, I put it into one of my internal / private mindmaps.

When I want to share a collection of knowledge with clients or others, I will sometimes make a mindmap public. Here are my public mindmaps: www.mindmeister.com/users/channel/georgekao

Have you tried mind mapping? If not, give it a go, and see if you enjoy organizing your knowledge that way.

My favorite mind mapping tool is MindMeister.

For an unlimited free mindmapping alternative, try MindMup, but it has fewer features than MindMeister.

Articles (or blog posts)

This is the most common format for sharing online content.

If writing is natural or easy for you, then I highly recommend that you write blog posts and share them to social media. One advantage to articles is that it's easy for search engines to understand and therefore index your text, allowing more people to find you.

The drawback to this content strategy is that many people find writing to be natural or easy, so it's harder to rise above the crowd in terms of quality.

However, I do believe that quantity can lead to quality: write more, and inevitably some of your writing will be excellent and shared forward by your readers.

Courses

An online course is usually a collection of videos and documents, with a step by step curriculum in mind, and specific results the students can expect to achieve. Think of an online course as a combination of different content formats.

Some online courses provide ample interaction with instructors, such as through live Q&A calls and/or a private online forum or facebook group.

Other online courses are completely DIY and "evergreen" (i.e. students can enroll anytime and go through the course at their own pace.)

Udemy is the most popular platform for online courses, with millions of students and tens of thousands of online courses, many of them free.

An up and coming competitor to Udemy is Skillshare.

If online courses interest you, consider uploading your course to both Udemy and Skillshare. At this time, they do not require exclusivity, i.e. you can sell your Udemy courses on your own website too.

The **benefit** of Udemy and Skillshare is that they have lots of students on the platforms already, and by putting your content there, some of those students will find you through their search engine and directory.

The **drawback** to such platforms is that you don't get access to your students' email address. You cannot freely email them through the platform, except to clarify something about the course. In other words, you can't expect to sell other products and services to students who take your courses, or even build your email list, through such platforms. If you want more control, put the course on your own website instead, using tools such as Thinkific or Teachable.

Social media posts

A lot of people take it for granted, but posting things on social media *is* content creation and sharing!

You can post short status updates or long articles. Short videos, or long lectures. Photos from your life, or image quotes.

Popular social media platforms include:

- Facebook (more than 2 billion users, and the most popular platform for every age group and every income level)

- Twitter (great for short updates, sharing links or photos)

- LinkedIn (not just an online rolodex but now a content platform too)

- Instagram (for images)

- SnapChat (images with filters, and sharing short videos)

- Google Plus (helpful for SEO)

My recommendation is to find one or two social media platforms you really enjoy using. That will make it more personally-sustainable for you to create and share content consistently.

Since I teach marketing, I use more social media platforms than a normal person. Here are my profiles:

- FB Business Page: www.FB.com/GeorgeKaoCommunity
- FB Personal Page: www.FB.com/GeorgeKao
- LinkedIn Profile: www.linkedin.com/in/GeorgeKao
- Google Plus: www.google.com/+GeorgeKaoCommunity
- Twitter: www.twitter.com/GeorgeKao
- Instagram: www.instagram.com/GeoKao

eBooks

This is usually a PDF download on a website.

However, if you're going to go through the effort of writing an e-book, and it's at least 3,000 words (preferably 5,000 or more), why not also publish it to the Amazon Kindle?

Books

If you are a coach, consultant, speaker, healer, or otherwise wish to build a personal brand, it seems to me that books are still the best credibility builder, especially if you put in the work to write a good book.

After the writing is done, it is now easy to self-publish, and I would recommend self-publishing as a way to test whether your book will have traction. Once your book does well, then you might approach (or be approached) by a publisher to take the book to the next level.

You can self-publish paperback books using Amazon's CreateSpace program, or soon using Amazon KDP -- https://kdp.amazon.com/en_US/help/topic/AH8RA6CMVRN8Y -- that is, publishing to Kindle first, then easily publishing to paperback format.

You can hire people affordably on Fiverr.com to format your content for CreateSpace. See here: http://bit.ly/2twiHi3

Speaking in-person

In-person speaking is, I believe, the most powerful "format" of content in terms of transforming audiences, and building a deep and memorable connection.

This can include in-person lectures, trainings, keynotes, workshops, and retreats.

**

Ultimately, what format your content gets packaged into, is limited only by your creativity and technology. Here are more ideas of content formats: www.medium.com/@georgekao/offer-formats-dacb6bf576be

Any questions about content formats? Comment here:
www.FB.com/GeorgeKaoCommunity/posts/10154758638669867

Chapter 6: Which content format is right for you?

What type of content should you create? Blog posts, videos, podcasts, infographics?

1. Start with the question *"What's more natural for me?"*

Do you enjoy writing? (Then commit to a rhythm of blog posts that you share to social media; your blog posts can eventually be edited into a book!)

Do you prefer to talk out your ideas? (Then record videos and post them to YouTube and Facebook, or record audio podcasts and put it on iTunes and Google Play.)

Do what's natural for you first. You can always repurpose that content later into a different format.

See more about "repurposing" content here:
www.FB.com/GeorgeKaoCommunity/posts/10154881385509867

2. What have you seen your niche mates do, that you're energized to learn to do also?

For example, some people have enjoyed my casual short videos that I take on my dog walks, and that got them going on their own videos too.

Or maybe you've enjoyed your niche mates' blog posts, and you believe that you also could contribute just as well by writing articles.

3. Ask your ideal clients: what format do they prefer to consume?

Simply email them with a short list of your favorite formats, and ask them what they're most likely to consume, and what they think is the best fit for you.

4. Try out various formats.

Ultimately, the best way is to try sharing your message in different formats, and see where you get the best feedback!

Chapter 7: What to say in your content?

Now that you have selected some way of creating content that feels natural to you, what do you say?

In this chapter, I offer you a variety of ways to help you create your messages. Consider each one. Try them out. The only way to discover your *authentic content creation* method is to experiment. Observe what you enjoy, and what your ideal audience likes the most.

As marketing guru Seth Godin says, "Don't go around insisting that you made something remarkable... Instead, test different things you made, and see what your audience likes the best."

Method #1. Pause for Ideas after Your Client Sessions

During each client session you have, observe your client's transformation. There's usually some "aha!" moment, or some story of progress they share with you Also, notice what questions they ask you.

Your clients' questions can be turned into useful content.

Try this on as a new habit: After you meet with a client, take a moment to pause, and write down the *key ideas*, *process*, or *examples* you shared, that your client found to be helpful.

I make this habit easier by having this simple form to fill out:

What results or progress did they celebrate?

What questions did they ask? (and solutions you gave?)

What exercise did you lead them through, if any?

What "aha!" moment did they have, if any?

What assignments did you give them, if any?

You might want to create a Google Form (a free online tool) with the above questions, and bookmark it so you can easily fill it out after each session.

Then once a week, I go and look at the form and see what I filled out the past week. I ask myself which idea I would like to turn into some piece of content.

If you're feeling especially inspired about a client session, you could immediately record a video or write a quick blog post.

For confidentiality purposes, change the name and details, so that no reader can identify the person you are talking about.

Client Stories / Case Studies

Once you've gotten some notes about how your clients transform as a result of working with you, it is useful to create Case Studies.

These case studies / stories can be placed into your content when appropriate, or included as part of your website copy.

Here is the basic structure of a Case Study:

Part 1. What is your client coming to you with, the problems they are facing as they begin the work with you? What challenges got them to seek you out? Was there a triggering event that motivated them to seek out someone like you? What hopes and dreams did they believe they could achieve by working with you?

Part 2. What work are you doing with them? What modality are you using, what tools, exercises, processes? Describe it briefly, so the reader has a basic sense of what you do with clients.

Part 3. What are their reactions and insights as they work with you? Is there something they were initially confused by, then became enlightened with? What was their greatest "aha!" moment? What part of the work with you did they love most?

Part 4. What is the result / transformation from working with you? Describe specifics. Imagine a movie scene in their life, before and after working with you. Describe the contrast. Give details that illustrate the transformation.

NOTE: The story doesn't have to be perfect, nor have great grammar, nor be very compelling. Just something written for now is fine. You can always improve upon it later.

As you write your case studies, memorize the best ones, and the common threads among them. This will be very useful whenever you work on your marketing, or whenever you're describing your service to someone.

Method #2. Get Interviewed

I'm not talking about getting on some famous TV show, although if you're invited, you might want to say "Yes" :-)

What I mean by "get interviewed" is that usually, *we have an easier time answering other people's questions, than trying to come up with content by ourselves in isolation.*

So reach out to someone, and have them meet with you for 15 minutes, longer if possible. Have them ask you about your work, and the issues you work on with clients.

Who might be happy to interview you? Some ideas:

- Your clients

- Friend who is supportive of your work
- Kindred spirit that you meet in a Facebook group such as as Awarepreneurs -- you can swap interviews with people. See Awarepreneurs here:
  www.FB.com/groups/awarepreneurs

You might want to send your interviewer 2 or 3 suggested questions in advance. Encourage them to take the conversation wherever they want to go, into whatever sub-topic that piques their curiosity. Let them know that the purpose is to pull out of you some thoughts that could become blog posts or videos.

As for the technology, the simplest way is via phone, Skype, or Zoom.

This type of interview can also be done over an email thread, back and forth... or even over text messaging. Pick a method that is natural for you, and for them.

Method #3. Comment in Groups

Is there an online group that you like to hang out in?

If you see a thread where you could contribute your wisdom, especially from your area of expertise (the topic of your business), by all means, comment on those threads!

Kind of like being interviewed, you're more likely to create content naturally when you engage in a discussion, than when trying to write alone.

What are people asking about, or discussing, with emotion or fascination? Show up in the relevant online forums and groups with curiosity and empathy, and you will discover plenty of ideas that can turn into relevant content for you.

If you already like to comment on Facebook, you can go to the following link to find all of your own Facebook comments: www.FB.com/me/allactivity?privacy_source=activity_log&log_filter=cluster_116

Method #4. Summarizing an Article or Book

If you enjoy reading books in your field, why not take some notes, and share your learnings with your audience?

By doing this, you reinforce your learning, and you help your audience.

And, because the piece of content will have the book title and author's name included, your content will be more likely to be found on search engines.

My book summary videos have been watched more than most of my other videos, because readers are typing in the book titles into the search engine, and sometimes, they find my content as a result.

(Note: I haven't done book summary videos in a long time, because I've been focused on creating my own content, and writing my books.)

Method #5. Outdoor Videos

I walk my dog daily. (One of the benefits of having a dog is it forces you to exercise more!)

When I arrive at the dog park, I'm sometimes just standing around, waiting for my dog Buddy to run around, play, and sniff.

One day I decided to pull out my phone and record a quick video message of inspiration for my clients.

The rest is history... I now have more than a hundred video messages, most of which are from my dog walks, where I share tips about heart-based business, marketing, and life.

You can see them all here: www.GeorgeKao.com/videos

**

Which of these 5 natural ways of creating content might work for you?

Feel free to comment here:

www.FB.com/GeorgeKaoCommunity/posts/10154838767789867

Getting Comfortable with Making Videos

In 2009, I made my first video. Then, I didn't make another video for 4 years. What happened?

I saw my first video and said... "George, wow you're ugly, and your voice sounds bad. What do you think, you're some movie star? People don't need to see you on video!"

It was these self-deprecating thoughts that kept me from doing video for years.

Then, in 2013, some friends encouraged me to try video again. I made a short video for them. They were supportive.

You, too, can start this way: Send your first video to a very small number of supportive friends and say that you're trying to get comfortable doing video, and would love their encouragement!

Later, I did a live video for a small portion of my audience, mentioning that I was trying to get comfortable doing video. They were also supportive, too. (So after you've shared with a small number of friends first, then share your video on your Facebook profile, and ask for your network's encouragement and support!)

These days, I'm very comfortable on video, because of all the practice and support. You can get there too.

I now focus on my message and my connection with my audience -- it is more important than what I might think about my own appearance.

You will get there as well, if you are willing to learn this key lesson: first make a video for a tiny group of supportive friends. Let them encourage you. *Then gradually expand the circle of people invited to watch your videos.*

In 2015, I made a commitment to create 100 videos. I learned a great deal by meeting that commitment. To see my favorite video tips, click on this comprehensive blog post: www.bit.ly/GKvideotipsonmedium

Advanced Method: Interview your Ideal Clients and Gather Tips

Here is a way to create valuable content, that also helps you to meet people who might refer you to future clients:

Interview people who are similar to your ideal clients, and distill those interviews into tips that will be helpful to your ideal client.

You can do this with the following steps:

STEP 1. Think about who your ideal clients are. Bring them to mind. Write down their names if that will help.

Now, think about the main problem that you help your ideal clients solve... let's call that "Problem X." Write it down.

Look at your contacts and network: Facebook friends, LinkedIn network, your email or phone contacts. Who do you know has made *some* progress (any progress) into solving Problem X?

Truly, everyone who is your ideal client has made *some* inroads into solving Problem X, even if they don't think they're successful at it yet.

Find 10 such people from your network.

STEP 2. Reach out to those people via individual messaging, such using email, text, or Facebook Messenger.

Let them know that you are putting together an in-depth article that gathers together some of the current strategies people are using to solve Problem X, and would they be willing to contribute a tip or two?

Ask for permission to use their full name (and profession, if appropriate), or just the first letter of their last name, or if they prefer to remain completely anonymous.

The benefits to them include:

1. They get to help others who are at an earlier stage than they are (Good karma!)

2. You'll be putting together the best tips you find, and sharing that article with them, which they are welcome to share forward if they have friends who would be helped by it.

3. If they are open to receiving advice, you'll offer your own thoughts about how they specifically could be more effective in solving Problem X.

4. You'd be happy to introduce them to anyone else that you interviewed, if they would like to keep in touch for mutual support, for example.

Side note: I think "getting visibility" for the interviewee is _not_ a legitimate benefit for an article like this... even if it's often used as a bait to get interviewees to say yes. The above four benefits are legit.

Be sure to give a due date for when you need their tip(s) by.

It is also helpful to give them a format, so they don't have to think too hard. For example, have them fill in these sentences:

> "Thus far, the most helpful thing I've done to solve Problem X has been _____."
>
> "A misconception I had about solving Problem X was: _____."
>
> "If I were helping someone who is a year earlier than me in solving Problem X, here's what else I would say to them: _____."

STEP 3. If they are responsive and helpful, take the conversation further. Ask details about the tip(s) they shared. And if it feels appropriate, also share a few of your own opinions / ideas for how they specifically might be more effective in solving Problem X.

Ask if they have any friends or colleagues that would be good to interview as well, that they'd be happy to introduce you to.

NOTE: Once you've gathered some interviews, you can go back to those who did not originally say yes to you, but that you'd really like to interview, and let them know that you've already gotten X number of interviewees. If you're approaching companies, let them know which companies have already said yes, if you're allowed to name them. Offer them the opportunity one more time.

STEP 4. Gather all the tips you get. Arrange them into themes. Write your article!

(By this point it might even be a little eBook you're writing!)

Here's an important key -- be sure to also share **your own opinions** throughout the article. This is one of the complaints I have about "expert roundup posts"... the curator isn't giving us any indication of which tips they would particularly recommend, and what else they would say about solving Problem X.

Be a more opinionated curator, so that your audience can witness your expertise as well.

STEP 5. Share the draft of your article/eBook with the ones who responded, letting them know which part of the article you quoted them or shared their idea... and ask if they have any edits they'd like you to make.

Give a due date for receiving their edits.

STEP 6. Gather all the edits and make final changes.

STEP 7. Put the article on your blog. Contact your interviewees with a *sincere thank you.*

Let them know you'll be sharing the article soon, but if they'd like to be one of the first to share this valuable article (people on social media love what is current and new!) then they are welcome to.

Let them know which date you'll start sharing the article more widely.

On that date, do as you promised and share the article to your email subscribers and on all the social media platforms you use... and for the interviewees who didn't mind being mentioned, be sure to tag or mention them, with gratitude!

Plan to share that article again in 1-4 weeks, because worthwhile content should be distributed multiple times, even on the same platform. People often need to see something more than once or twice before they decide to click it.

STEP 8. Take the relationships with your supportive interviewees to the next level, however you feel appropriate.

Ideas include:

- Connecting particular interviewees whom you think would benefit from knowing each other. (First check with each person before you make the intro!)

- Consider gathering a mastermind of interviewees, to continue solving Problem X, and you could facilitate that mastermind short-term (2-5 sessions), or longer term. If it seems appropriate for you and them, you could even charge a fee for this.

- If there was an interviewee that was particularly responsive to your advice, reach out and see if they would like to continue getting your service (coaching, consulting, healing, etc.) -- maybe for some kind of deal given that they were helpful for your article... e.g. a discount on the first session, or a bonus gift of some kind.

If you found this strategy interesting, I encourage you to give it a go!

Watch the companion short video and comment on this strategy in this FB post:
www.FB.com/GeorgeKaoCommunity/videos/10156140984894867

Advanced Method: Social Media Research

Another method is to create content based on what your ideal clients are posting on social media.

Think about it -- when your clients share an article on social media, it's because they think it's worth sharing. Well, if you create an article (or a video) like that, might they also be more likely to share it? Yes.

Start by observing *what your clients are sharing on social media.*

> What links, articles, videos, images, are they sharing on Facebook, Instagram, Twitter, LinkedIn, or wherever you and they both use social media?

Of everything they share, what's related to some part of your Framework? (See the chapter later on Transformational Framework.)

Regarding these pieces of content, ask these 3 questions:

- What do I disagree with and could offer my perspective on?
- What do I agree with that can be said in my own style?
- What related important idea was missing in that article or video?

Then, create your own version of the content -- addressing the same question or topic, but from *your* perspective, expertise, and experience. You will be creating content that your clients and prospective clients want, but in your own voice.

Advanced Method: Keyword Research

What are your "keywords"? Think of it this way... when your ideal clients use a search engine to find solutions to the problems you help them solve, what phrases, what questions would they type into the search engine?

Write articles (and make videos) that answer questions that your ideal clients are typing into the search engines. What they're typing in, is what we call your "keywords".

A "keyword" is usually not just one word, but a question or a phrase.

The more you get clear on keywords, and create content based on those, the more your SEO (search engine optimization) will rock.

Keywords are not in your jargon, but in the audience's language.

Step 1. Write the potential words or questions that ideal clients might type into a search engine.

Write out at least 25 that are related to your services, what you do for clients, and most importantly, what questions they ask you.

Step 2. Prioritize these keywords based on what you would most like your website to be found on. If there were just 5 keywords you want to really champion, that you really want people to think of you for, what are those 5? Again, these could be client problems stated as questions, or brief phrases.

Step 3. Go to www.google.com and start typing in your top keywords and notice what the auto-complete suggests. Choose the most relevant one.

Notice the content that comes up on the first page of the search results. (Not the advertisements, but the organic search results.)

This is what your prospective clients are finding when they google that keyword.

The reason those links are showing up on the first page of the search results is because those links are what people tend to be clicking, and what influencers are referring other people to (by linking to those articles on their own website).

If you can improve upon any of the pieces on the first page of the search results, you will be on the winning side. If you could improve upon any of those top pieces of content, you could have excellent and findable content, assuming you then do the work of distributing that content.

Yes, I'm aware of the Google Keyword Planner (part of the Google Adwords platform.) I've used it myself, and helped clients to use it. However, compared to the benefits it offers, it is more complicated and unnecessary for most of the people in my audience. You don't need it to build a winning content strategy -- not yet. I strongly recommend using my simpler method for now.

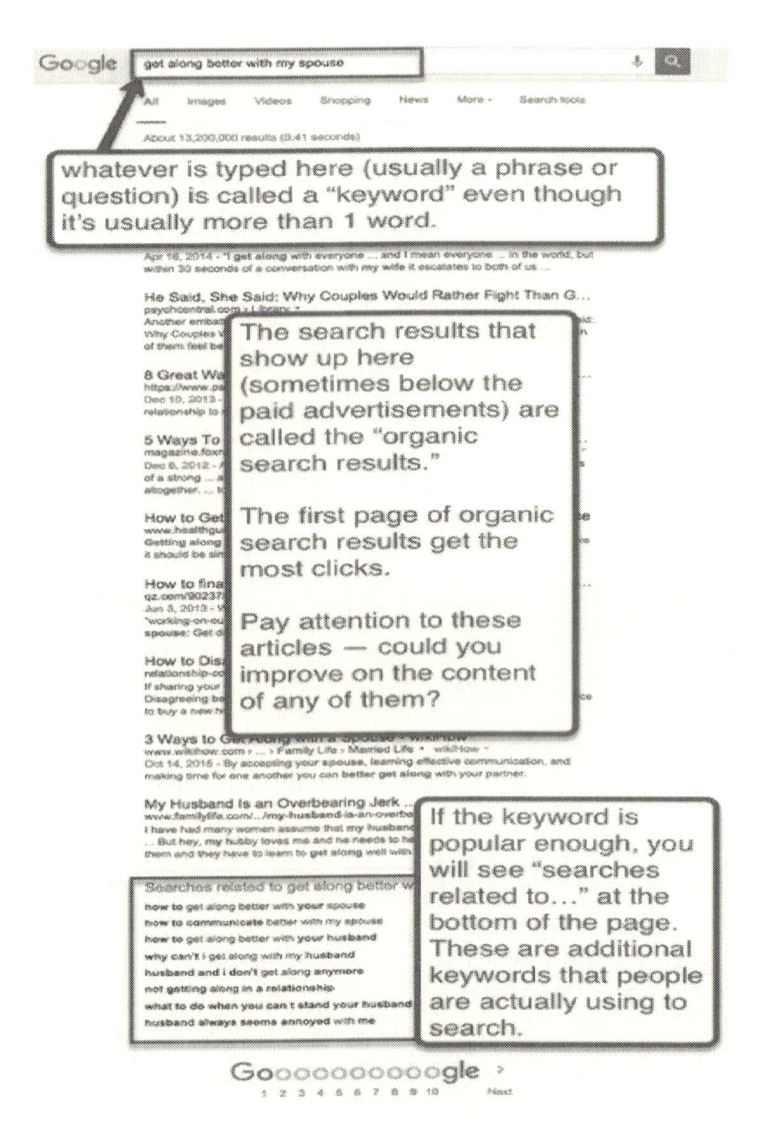

[Screenshot of a Google search for "get along better with my spouse" with annotations:]

- whatever is typed here (usually a phrase or question) is called a "keyword" even though it's usually more than 1 word.
- The search results that show up here (sometimes below the paid advertisements) are called the "organic search results."
- The first page of organic search results get the most clicks.
- Pay attention to these articles — could you improve on the content of any of them?
- If the keyword is popular enough, you will see "searches related to..." at the bottom of the page. These are additional keywords that people are actually using to search.

- Notice the "related searches" (bottom) section that offers additional keywords.

Step 4. For each of your top keywords, create an article that integrates the information from the first page of search results... aim to be even more useful than the links that the search engine is displaying.

As you write your article, ask these questions regarding the top articles:

- What do I disagree with, that I can offer my perspective on?

- What do I agree with, that I could say in my own way?

- What related idea, example, or perspective is missing, yet important?

Remember: search engines want to be as useful to people as possible... if you help them achieve that with your website, your site will be ranked well.

Repeat Step 3 and Step 4 with each keyword that you want to be known for. By doing this, you are creating highly relevant content.

And, as you write articles, you can eventually integrate them into a book! For example, just 5,000 words is totally acceptable for a Kindle book, if it is a helpful and/or inspiring book for your ideal audience.

Focus your content on being one of the experts in your field, by understanding your ideal clients' keywords, and creating content about it.

Chapter 8: How I overcame many years of writer's block

In the beginning of the book, I mentioned that I hated writing most of my life, and only overcame this in the past few years. Here's how I did it...

In 2015, I was one year into my business awakening (which I will write about someday!) and I decided to challenge myself to make five casual videos a week.

Once I started making videos, I realized that many people prefer to read instead of take the time to watch a talking-head video. In fact, I'm the same way... reading is much faster to get the ideas than sitting through a video.

So, out of courtesy, I started to quickly, casually, write out the content of my videos.

I thought, "I'm just going to quickly type what I basically said in the video, so those who don't watch can still get the message."

I started doing this before bed, on my little iPhone screen. Interestingly, having such a small screen eased my writer's block for 2 reasons:

1. Just a few sentences, typed out, made it look on a small screen like I was writing a lot, which increased my confidence.

2. Letters appearing across the small screen, as I typed, looked like I was writing faster than it would've looked on a computer screen.

Because I was making five videos a week (one each weekday), I had to do the writing five days a week as well, and I found it was always at the same time -- right before bed.

(Now, my writing rhythm has changed to 3 days a week, 8:30am - 9am.)

A few dozen videos and writings later, I came to realize that *I had overcome my writer's block!*

I did this without *trying* to overcome the block... but simply as a result of these factors:

1. I was writing very casually, without thinking "this is going to be a blog post / book." It would have been too intimidating for me at the time. "No big deal; this is just a quick summary of my video," and that was the key to overcoming my perfectionism. This allowed me to finally share my writing, and to keep doing it.

2. I was writing in a medium that didn't intimidate me: my iPhone. It felt like I was writing a quick email to a friend. If I had been writing on my computer, with a blank screen staring at me, I would have been too anxious. For some people, instead of writing on the phone, it helps to open up a new email message on the computer, and write as if to a supportive friend. You don't have to try to impress them or perform through your writing; you are just enjoying that connection with them, and sharing your thoughts honestly.

3. I was writing content almost everyday, which became a daily practice of ignoring any fear/anxiety that might overtake me. Years later, I still feel some fear, doubt, and perfectionism every time I write. (In fact, **right now** I feel these as I write this to you!) But the muscle of *ignoring those feelings* has grown very strong. Instead, I pay attention to the excitement of exploring my message and the joy of sharing them with you, and I focus on the feelings of service and connection.

4. I was writing at the same time everyday. This had the effect of priming my brain: "It's time to write!"

5. Since I was posting all my writing on social media, I was getting appreciation for at least some of it, which was enough to encourage me to keep going.

6. I had accountability. My audience was now expecting to see my writing on a regular schedule. I didn't want to let them down. I don't want to let *you* down.

In summary:

- Write casually
- Write in a medium that prevents anxiety (e.g. emailing a supportive friend)
- Grow your muscle of ignoring negative feelings, attending to positive ones
- Write at the same time each day
- Share it with supportive people first
- Get accountability (private or public) if that helps you

If I can dissolve 30+ years of writer's block, you can as well. Try the factors listed above and see how it helps you.

To receive my best writings, via email, once a month, check out my free newsletter:
www.GeorgeKao.com/Newsletter

Writing tools

When you need to get unstuck in your writing, try this free tool:

www.themostdangerouswritingapp.com

Just write stream-of-consciousness for a few minutes. Make no judgment or evaluation. Don't stop. Just write whatever comes out. You can always edit it later! For now, just get into the rhythm of typing.

Here are additional writing tools that my clients have liked:

- Scrivener: complicated to start using, but once you learn it, can be very helpful for writing books. I'm not using it, but some of my clients swear by it.

- HemingwayApp: a free app to help you write in a more readable way.

- Grammarly: a powerful grammar-checker.

Chapter 9: Your Transformational Framework

Now that you've gotten some experience creating content, by following some of the methods in this book, it's time to take it to the next level.

Ultimately, what should be at the core of your Content is your *Transformational Framework.*

What is the overall process or journey through which you lead your clients?

Perhaps it's a process you've designed from your own life experience, or from helping others. It might also be a combination of various trainings you've done, and the many books you've read.

Your framework could also be based on what you've learned from a teacher/mentor, or from a particular school of thought.

However you came to your Transformational Framework, once you clarify the various pieces of it, you have an abundant source of relevant content ideas.

Content that is created from your Transformational Framework will help your current clients, and draw to you many more ideal clients.

You can talk about each piece of your Framework through articles or videos.

After you've created content about each piece of your Framework, cycle back to the start and create more. Each time you cycle back, create content with different examples or a new point of view, related to your current experience, or something happening in the world.

For example, it takes me at least six months to create & share content for the various pieces of my Framework. Then I start over again, this time with six months' of new experiences, clients, and things that have happened in my industry (or in the world) that I can comment about, as related to my content.

There are 3 elements of a Transformational Framework:

The Forest

The "forest" is the overall method of how you facilitate your clients' transformation.

What are the basic steps you take a new client through, from the circumstances and issues that they have, to having those issues fully resolved?

What is the process you handhold your clients through, to being completely transformed?

Examples include:

- Don Miguel Ruiz's "Four Agreements"
- Byron Katie's "The 4 Questions and Turnarounds"
- Stephen Covey's "7 Habits of Highly Effective People"
- Alcoholics Anonymous "12 Step Program" for addiction recovery

Here is my own framework, "The Authentic Business"...

1. There are 5 areas that an authentic business needs to create and continually improve:
    a. Content (what this book is about)
    b. Product (the match between your product/services and your market)

c. Connections (authentic networking and mindful joint ventures)
   d. Productivity (improving how you manage your time, information, energy)
   e. Clients (enrolling new clients and inspiring current clients to refer you)

2. There are ongoing principles that apply to all areas:
   a. Vision that Energizes You
   b. Focus on Your Strengths in all areas
   c. Kaizen (continuous experimentation and improvement)
   d. Be a <u>Big Picture Perfectionist</u> not a small perfectionist
   e. Always be Honest and Caring

This is a very simplified version of the framework that I've created, and use daily, to handhold my clients through creating their own thriving, authentic business.

It is also the outline I use to create new content.

What about your transformational framework? How many steps does it have?

Before I offer some tips on how to figure out the steps of your Framework, let me share with you the overall picture. The next idea is "trees".

The Trees

If each step or part of your Framework is like sections of a forest, then the individual trees are the various specific tools:

- Specific terms/concepts that clients must learn
- Specific processes through which you walk your clients
- Specific practices and exercises that you recommend clients do

- Specific projects that clients must accomplish (or that you do for them)
- Detailed problems that you help clients solve

Within each Step, there are usually at least 1 or more of the above specific things.

For example, "Content" is one of the major steps of my Framework, and the specific tools and ideas include:

- 3 Stages of Content
- 5 Methods for Creating Content Naturally
- The Transformational Framework
- (in fact, you can just look at the table of contents of this book, to see the specific tools of the Content part of my framework!)

The Ecosystem

Lastly, how does your framework differ from other frameworks?

It's not that yours is better than everyone else's.

We wouldn't say that the ecosystem of a forest is "better" than that of an ocean. They are simply different, and serve different beings. A monkey might thrive in a forest, yet drown in the ocean. A fish thrives in the ocean, and would suffocate in a forest.

Similarly, your ideal clients thrive within your framework, and might suffocate in someone else's. And yet, someone else might thrive in your niche mate's framework, and drown in yours. Different frameworks serve different people, and that is a good thing.

Get clear on _why_ other solutions are _not_ a good fit for your ideal clients. This is where studying the other businesses (and frameworks) in your industry can be helpful. Through contrast, you come to see how your framework is unique, and for whom it is most beneficial.

For example, my Authentic Business framework isn't a good match for all entrepreneurs. It is, however, a wonderful match for my ideal clients, who are spiritually-oriented service providers who have a transformational message/method to offer the world.

Those who don't resonate with my "spiritual" language, or businesses that are selling a product mainly because of profit (rather than as a Calling) are best served by more mainstream business consultants. It's not that my framework is "better". It is simply a different ecosystem that serves a different type of person. Biodiversity is a good thing!

Everyone can be served. Every business can thrive, if we all focus our offerings on those who can most thrive in our ecosystem.

Steps for Creating Your Transformational Framework

1. Brainstorm all the various things you do with your ideal clients, or would like to do:
    a. What skills do you teach them?
    b. What exercises do you walk them through?
    c. What specific projects do you help them accomplish?
    d. What specific issues do you handhold them through?

2. Group them into topics, using an Outline or Mindmap.

3. Add items as needed.

4. Remove items if they're unnecessarily duplicative.

5. Move items around if they work better under a different topic.

6. Name each topic, or tool, something unique if possible, unless it's already well-loved tool/name you're using from someone else.

7. Reality is ineffable, so know that your Framework can, and will, change over time. I find myself updating my framework (sometimes dramatically) every 2-3 years, based on the new important factors in the business world, and in my own experience.

FAQs About Your Framework

Look carefully at your framework, and answer the following questions.

(If you don't have any clients yet, then answer these questions about your ideal/prospective clients.)

- What questions do clients typically ask you?
- What questions or challenges are going through their mind?
- What mistakes are they making as they try to reach their goals?
- What terms or ideas would they want more clarity on?
- Would they ask how certain ideas are relevant to their life?
- Would they ask how an idea is related to a current event or trend?
- What are common obstacles or problems they encounter in each step?

Write as many questions as you can... then prioritize the questions from most likely to be asked, to least likely.

Then, create content that answers these questions, from your perspective and style.

Also, integrate the top questions into your marketing. For example, on your homepage, on your Services page, in your LinkedIn Summary section, on your Facebook Business Page... so that your audience might think of You as the go-to person about these questions.

As an example, one of my clients -- Michelle M. Olsen of GreenLight Coaching -- is a career coach, and one of the frequently-asked questions she gets from clients is "Should I quit my current job?" As a

result, she created this blog post & video to answer that question, from her perspective and framework:
www.FB.com/GreenLightCoaching/posts/10158707712870597

Chapter 10: Which content should be Free versus Paid?

In 2014 I promoted the idea that "all content should be free" because it would (1) help humanity progress faster, (2) help you attract your ideal audience, and (3) make you more creative by easing the pressure to make your content perfect.

I've continued to evolve my stance since then. Here's what I believe now:

Free content should be easy to consume: nothing complicated or requiring thoughtful implementation.

If a piece of knowledge you want to transmit, takes a substantial amount of energy for the reader/viewer to parse and understand, it makes sense for the viewer to spend some money (doesn't have to be a lot) to signal to themselves, and to you, that they are ready to invest some energy into making that knowledge work for them.

If gyms were free, there would be a lot fewer people who actually use them.

Even better is if paid content can be packaged as a live experience -- where the student is required to "show up" -- in order to consume that content.

Still, I believe that paid content should be as affordable as possible, since it is a scalable revenue source. Make it accessible to as many income brackets as possible. They don't have to invest a lot of money to be willing to invest their energy into integrating that content. They just have to pay something.

This year, I have been offering my $25, two-hour live online workshops, where the recording is only available to those who attend.

Attendance has been steadily high. Whereas free webinars usually have 15-35% attendance (e.g. out of 100 people who register, only 15-35 attend), my paid online workshops are getting an average of 92% attendance! (Out of every 100 registrants, 92 show up!)

It's not because of the high price that people show up. (There's a mis-truth being taught out there that the "more" money someone spends, the "more" they show up. I have sold $2,000 online courses, and $25 workshops, and have found no correlation between attendance and price.)

People show up because I teach on a topic they want, and ask them to sign up only if they intend to show up.

Do I still believe that in the long run, all content should be free?

Yes, as a long-term, *lifetime project.*

I aim to eventually make every piece of knowledge I have, free. As I figure out how to make each piece entertaining and easy to consume, I make it free.

Until then, I share for free that which is easily consumable, and I charge for the rest: as affordable, online learning events.

Note: even if you make all your content free, the interesting thing is that your audience will still want to buy your paid information products if those products (books, courses) are a thoughtfully curated, edited version of your free content.

For example, most of this entire book is freely available on my social media profiles, if you were willing to go through a few years of my videos & posts. Here in this book, you get it in an organized, edited format.

I'm not the only one who is saying this. Prolific content creators such as Seth Godin and Gary Vaynerchuk all sell books that are essentially a curated collection of their best free content. And their books sell very well.

The more free, good content you create and distribute online, the more people discover you and will buy your book or course.

**

In 2014 I also said that I don't believe content should be copyrighted.

That is still my stance today.

In my experience of working with over 1,000 clients, most of whom are "messengers" such as authors, experts, speakers, consultants, and coaches, I have seen far too much energy *wasted* in trying to "protect" copyrighted content.

The truth I've seen is that no matter how much you try to protect your content, those who want to share it illegally *will find a way to share it...* it doesn't matter if you give your students a login password -- it's easy for them to share it with friends, if they wanted to.

However, when you stop worrying about protecting your content, you *liberate* a lot of your energy towards *creating* instead!

You'll find that you actually have an infinite well, within your mind and heart, of creativity. You'll discover that there are always new ways of formulating and expressing your message. With a liberated energy, you'll keep uncovering new messages to give.

It's like with every 1 ounce of energy you liberate from not having to "protect" content, you'll find 2 ounces of new energy for creating.

You are a creator.

To add your comment about this chapter, go here:
www.FB.com/GeorgeKao/posts/10106478685618893

Keep your free content "white belt"

Whenever possible, keep your free content as "white belt" as possible... that is, easy to consume, not requiring much mental investment from the audience.

Think of a martial arts dojo. In any given beginner (white belt) class, you often see a few dedicated "black belt" students practicing the same basic moves... except that the black belts are practicing at a deeper, more nuanced level.

Advanced students know how important the basics are, and therefore they review them frequently.

Therefore, make most of your free content "white belt" because even "black belt" audience members will appreciate consuming beginner's content. They will see the deeper nuances that the beginners aren't.

In regard to your "black belt" content -- the stuff that is more in-depth, complex, or difficult to implement -- I recommend keeping them in your paid programs, workshops, courses, and books.

When students / clients have paid for these, they are more ready to get serious and invest the required energy to parse and understand your more advanced material.

However, you might aim to eventually convert all your advanced/complex topics into easily-consumable, white-belt content that can be shared for free. This is the mission that I'm on. It may take me another 10-15 years, but I hope to eventually give away all my ideas, even my most advanced ones, for free, by breaking them down into bite-sized, white-belt content.

When you're creating content, especially "white belt" stuff, see if you can include any example or case study to help illustrate or ground each idea.

With each piece of content, try to keep building on your Transformational Framework, so that eventually, your whole framework could be taught through many bite-sized pieces of content... which can eventually become Stage 2 content pieces, then eventually, Stage 3, such as your own book!

Chapter 11: The Path To Awesome Content

Do you yearn for your content to be well-loved, shared widely, and deeply impactful for your ideal audience?

The path to content quality is as follows...

1. Publish more content (e.g. articles, social media posts, videos, podcast episodes)

2. Notice which pieces of your content get shared & loved.

3. Bring those success factors into your future content.

Repeat this cycle as frequently as possible, and your content will become more engaging, loved by your audience, and naturally shared, without you having to ask.

In this chapter, I offer you my encouragement and instruction for applying yourself to this worthwhile path, as well as specific tips on how to create better content.

The Two Fantasies of Content Creators

First, let's explore 2 kinds of illusions that content creators suffer from...

1. Delusions of Content Grandeur: This happens whenever we are baffled why more people don't love our content as much as we do.

2. The Perfectionism Trap: This is when we have great taste, but know that our content falls far below that ideal standard, and thus we don't publish more content.

Which of these 2 problems do you experience?

I experience both, at different times.

How to solve these problems?

When suffering from *Delusion of Content Grandeur*, there are 2 possible reasons:

You aren't in-touch with your audience's sense of taste, and therefore, you need to create more content and observe what your audience likes.

The other possibility is that you aren't talking to your ideal audience yet! If you're not sure, then ask yourself who is buying (or most likely to buy) your services/products? Those are the people it makes sense to create your content for. That is your ideal audience.

If you don't have anyone buying your products/services yet, then you need to share your content to different audiences and see who responds the best to you.

Sometimes you'll also experience the second illusion I mentioned above: the *Perfectionism Trap*. You'll know you're experiencing this if you keep procrastinating on making & publishing content. You're waiting until you make the perfect thing before you share it.

You forgot that it takes a lot of practice *and* observation of feedback (which requires you to publish first!) in order to become better at content creation.

The Ugly Origami

Behavioral economist Dan Ariely describes an interesting study with 3 groups of people:

Group 1. People who were asked to build some origami without instructions... they had to figure it out themselves, tapping into their own creativity.

Group 2. People who were asked to build origami, but they were given step-by-step instructions.

Group 3. People who didn't build any origamis, but were asked to value (put a price on) each piece of origami that the other groups built.

It turns out that the builders (Groups 1 and 2) all valued their *own* pieces much more than the evaluators did!

Interestingly, the builders who didn't have instructions (Group 1) valued their own pieces *the most.* Since they had to figure it out by themselves, they felt most invested in the outcome.

This study points to the eternal illusion that we content creators experience...

Simply because we invest time and energy into creating something, whether it's a product, service, blog post, video, etc, we naturally come to believe that thing to be of much greater value, than our audiences who weren't involved in the building of it.

(One side lesson: involve your audience in the creation of something important!)

Our audiences are like the evaluators -- the third group in the study.

If we are not aware of our eternal blindness as creators, we get discouraged when our audience doesn't love our content as much as we do.

On the other hand, if we come to admit that this illusion is normal (it's certainly true for me) then we can have a different perspective about the creative process:

It's always about *testing our content*, not about "look at this great thing I've made!"

Don't invest so much in any marketing action you take. Instead, let yourself do *consistent, casual experimentation.*

We simply share with our audience what we have worked on -- and ideally share the drafts along the way -- so that we can observe the feedback and improve for the next round.

**

Maybe you've spent years studying a modality of healing/transformation and you think it's the most amazing process in the world.

And then, you share it with your audience, and you get silence. Blank stares.

It's not the modality or solution itself that sucks. It's not. It's more likely to be **how** you are describing it.

You've got to remember that all marketing is experimentation.

It's about trying one way of describing something. If that doesn't resonate, try another way.

All along the journey, observe your audience's wants and interests, and see how you can frame your marketing so that they resonate with it.

Again, the problem is that we don't really know what is good until we put it out there.

Share your content as often as possible. In this way, you will come to hone your intuition about what your audience wants to see from you.

You are welcome to comment on this chapter here:
www.FB.com/GeorgeKaoCommunity/posts/10154265923569867

The Parable of the Ceramics Class...

Whenever you'd like some inspiration to stop procrastinating and create content, read this...

The book "Art & Fear" has a wonderful story about a ceramics course — it can teach us about how to become great at what we do.

At the beginning of the week, a ceramics teacher divided her class in two groups of students.

The teacher instructed Group A to create *a large number* of pots. This group of students will be graded solely on the quantity of pots they produce. They don't have to worry about *quality*.

Each one simply has to *make as many pots as time allows*.

The students in Group B, on the other hand, were instructed to create *the perfect pot*. Each student in that group would be graded solely on the quality of the one pot that he or she made.

At the end of the week, both groups of students were instructed to put all their pots in one place.

The teacher, without knowing which pots came from which group, put the pots in order of their *quality*...

Interestingly, all the **highest quality** pots were made by students in Group A — that is, the *quantity* group, the students who made *as many pots as possible*.

Why did it happen this way? Why wasn't the Quality group able to make the highest quality pots?

It was because in the Quantity group, their goal was to make as many as possible, so they got a lot of experience with **the process** itself. They really learned how to work with the materials and the tools.

Importantly, they were practicing turning their ideas into reality...

...at first poorly, then better and better, more and more aligned to their vision.

Due to their experimentation, they had become more skilled by the day.

While the Quantity Group was busy creating, the Quality Group — the ones instructed to make just the "perfect" pot — was busy planning and designing the ideal pot... they were thinking a lot, but not really creating.

A lot of the Quality Group members had become paralyzed by the task... afraid of producing anything less than perfect...

I hope you'll learn this lesson well. When it comes to creating content, do you want to be in the Quantity or the Quality Group?

If you say Quantity group, how often should you be creating content? This is relative.

For some people, posting one thing a week is much more than they're already doing. That would be a good aim to start with.

For me, my rhythm currently is 3x a week, published to my Facebook Profile, Google Plus, LinkedIn, Twitter.

Seth Godin and Gary Vaynerchuk, two of the most respected business minds on the internet, recommend (and model) posting everyday.

Ultimately, the quantity strategy is about learning playfulness vs. seriousness... experimentation vs. perfection. Once we allow ourselves the freedom of expression that comes with knowing that each piece is a learning experience, then we can truly learn.

In other words, through *quantity*, we can come to *quality*.

Make lots of content, keep experimenting, post a lot. As you create & share many pieces, some of them you'll be especially proud of, and a few of them will be loved by your audience.

The problem is: you won't know which pieces your audience will find engaging. So the answer is *to publish more*.

Over the last few years of publishing content, I've become a content agnostic: I cannot predict with accuracy which of my pieces will do well. I'm "too close" to my own content. All I can do is humbly present my work and let my audience tell me what they love.

For some more encouragement on this, check out the following video that shares a powerful lesson by one of the top content creators of our era, Ira Glass of This American Life: www.bit.ly/2snmH5b

I've mentioned Seth Godin, one of the most successful content creators online. He has been blogging consistently (mostly daily) since 2002, and I noticed that it wasn't until about 2010 that (8 years later!) that his blog posts began to go viral.

He practices what he preaches: don't assume what you make is amazing. Make and publish more stuff and notice what your audience loves. Of course you don't have to take 8 years... if you follow the advice in this book, you'll shorten your learning curve by a lot!

> Don't go around insisting that you made something remarkable.
>
> Go around testing the different things you make, to see what your audience thinks is remarkable. ~ Seth Godin

Dangerous: Zero Engagement and Viral Content

When sharing your message, there are 2 situations that are dangerous to your creativity:

- When there is silence

- When it goes viral (gets popular)

When there's silence, you can get discouraged. What you thought was important or meaningful, others didn't bother to like, comment, or share.

I totally understand. I used to only share something if I felt it would be popular, and when it wasn't, I went for days (or weeks) without sharing any more content.

Now, I'm getting used to the cycles of silence (most of the time) and popularity (once in awhile. I simply share, knowing that likes/comments will come and go.

**

The second danger to our creativity is praise and admiration.

If your content gets liked and shared by many people, you can become scared about sharing the next thing... wanting it to be as well-loved as the previous piece.

And when the next thing doesn't get liked much, you feel discouraged, because you keep comparing it to the previous piece that went viral.

**

As you can see, both praise and lack thereof, can derail your creativity.

The solution?

Keep coming back to your higher purposes for creating and sharing: to grow yourself, to share what is worth sharing, and to positively impact others, if it is meant to be.

If you ground yourself in a spirit of service, your content becomes a mission, a cause.

You create and share consistently because it's worth doing, not because you are looking for praise.

When you do good for its own sake, you "win" every time you do it.

No matter the result, you can celebrate the action itself.

**

Only occasionally (e.g. monthly... not daily!) it is a good idea to look back at the content you shared that got the most praise, and ask "why might it be so?"

And look at content that got the least praise, and ask the same question.

By simply observing and asking these questions, you will naturally sharpen your intuition about what content is most engaging to your audience.

That will help you create better content going forward.

Again, don't look at your content metrics daily, but only occasionally. Distance creates perspective.

What is good to keep in mind daily is:

- "What idea would I like to explore today through content?"

- "What is worth sharing today?"

Then share good content, for its own sake.

You can comment on this post here:

www.FB.com/GeorgeKaoCommunity/posts/10154263870794867

Chapter 12: Practical Tips for Making Your Content Great

Hopefully by this point in the book, you believe that it's *the practice* of creating & publishing content, that will *eventually* make you a great content creator.

The question now: What skills to develop?

Practice your observation skills

1. Go to the social media profile (e.g. Facebook page) of your ideal clients. What are they sharing? If you also create/share that type of content, you are making what they might want to share. For example, if they share about a current trend, can you create content that applies your Framework to the current trend? If you keep doing this, your Framework becomes more understandable and interesting to your audience.

2. What content are your niche mates sharing? Of their pieces, which are getting the most engagement? Emulate that type of content. Advanced tip: observe the types of people engaging in your niche mates' content -- are they your ideal client types? Only take notice of what your ideal client types are engaging with.

What makes your content indispensable?

To have a loyal audience for your content, think about how to make it indispensable.

Here are 2 questions for you to work through...

1. My content is the best _____ ? (fill in the blank)

What are you genuinely excited to fill in that blank with? Options include:

- Would you like your content to contain the best research?
- Do you want to be the best teacher / create the best How-To content?
- Are you interested in making your content the highly entertaining? Funny?
- Does your content consistently have beautiful art, making it unique among your peers?
- Are you energized to have your content contain the most passion, compared to what others publish?
- Is your content the best for a particular type of person, or a particular stage of someone's journey?
- Does your content champion a particular worldview that you feel isn't expressed enough among your peers?

It will take some experimentation for you to become clear about your answer. How? Publish more, and observe the feedback.

As you come to understand what makes your content "better" than the content of your niche mates, in what way your content could be "the best", then focus on practicing those factors.

My example: I am working towards my content being *excellent marketing advice*, yet infused with a *deep caring* for my audience, *ethical values*, and a *spiritual worldview*. That makes it rare, and hopefully, indispensable for my ideal audience.

Here's the second question for you to answer:

2. Who is not getting the information they need to make improvements they want in their lives, work, or relationships?

For me, it would be holistic counselors, ethically-based consultants, and spiritually-oriented coaches. It's easy for them to find mainstream marketing/business advice, yet that advice is often devoid of true heart, values, or ethics. My audience would love to receive effective marketing guidance from someone whose values they can trust. I aim for my content to fill that market gap/niche.

What about you? Think about your ideal audience. What content are they already consuming, but are dissatisfied with?

I invite you to comment with your answers to either or both of the above questions here: www.FB.com/GeorgeKaoCommunity/posts/10154858204534867

The importance of emotions

This is one of my learning edges: eliciting emotions from my audience. A big reason I'm not so good at it, is because I am overly cautious about manipulating others. I want to genuinely share what I know…

However, I would be remiss if, in teaching marketing, I didn't bring up the importance of eliciting audience emotions.

The more you are able to influence (strong) emotions in your audience, the more they will remember your content, and the more they will share it forward.

Emotions that could emerge from your content include:

- Humor
- Beauty
- Anger
- Gratitude
- Fear
- Empathy

(I hope you'll steer away from trying to add more anger or fear in your audience… let's elicit positive emotions that inspire our audience to better their lives.)

In other words, try to add more "color", heart, or artistry into your content, and your audience will love it.

To do this consciously, without manipulating, you might take a moment, before you create content, and connect with the heart of your ideal audience member.

Imagine their state as they consume your content. Imagine how you'd like them to feel after consuming your content. Then, you'll more naturally add emotion & color into whatever you are creating.

Another way to do this is to imagine giving that content to a good friend of yours... how would you want to connect to your friend? When you tell a funny story to your friend, you naturally want to make them laugh, not out of manipulation but out of connection. Similarly, when you are instructing them, you want them to feel cared for.

Try to add more stories & examples into your content, as those tend to create more emotion because they connect with the experience of the reader.

No more fear-based headlines

Just because some marketing tactics "work" doesn't mean it's a good idea... it may bring more followers in the short-term, but erode your reputation in the long-term.

One such tactic is using fear-based headlines to make sure people click and read your stuff. Appeal to their fear of failure, fear of rejection, or fear of missing out. Yes, this "works" to get people to do stuff. This is what marketers often teach us. This is called "click bait".

As people who yearn for a better world, it is our calling to redefine what it means when something "works"... does it work for your higher self? Does it add Love and Wisdom?

I really liked the following comment from Rachel Heslin regarding such tactics:

"I agree that [fear-based headlines] can be very useful in getting people to read your stuff. At the same time, may I respectfully suggest a larger viewpoint? The world is about more than just getting people to read our stuff. While our focus may be on nurturing engagement, please consider the potential impact of those techniques which not only acknowledge, but deliberately attempt to foster and increase fear. There is more than enough fear in our world — just look at the current political campaigns! Fear causes tunnel vision, narrowing our ability to be creative and make conscious choices.

What if, instead, we chose our language and marketing with an eye towards raising the hopes and confidence of our readers? What if they were drawn to us because we *inspire* them? Each of us does what we think we need to do. I just think it important to point out that words can have power, and maybe we need to ask ourselves if we are using that power for greater good."

You can comment on this here: www.FB.com/GeorgeKaoCommunity/posts/10154707134764867

KISS

Basically, **K**eep **I**t **S**imple & **S**incere!

That's how you start.

You don't have to solve the world's problems in one blog post or video. Just give the ideal reader a few tips they can use right now. Be sincere about your thoughts on the matter.

Don't worry about becoming an Amazon Best Seller

For those of us who are interested in publishing books, have you wondered how to become an "Amazon Best Selling Author"?

Check out this shocking article:
"What does it take to be a bestselling author? $3 and 5 Minutes"
www.bit.ly/2sCubmL

Turns out that it's not difficult. It has been easy to game Amazon's system until now, and for the foreseeable future.

Regardless of whether you get that Best Seller badge, let's focus on writing books we are proud to share.

Chapter 13: How To Spread Your Content

You have spent the energy to write or record something.

But if you don't spend the energy to effectively distribute it to where your ideal audience is, who is going to see it, share it, or be impacted by it? No one.

Some content marketing experts are now recommending that we spend *as much effort* distributing/sharing our content, as we do in creating it.

What I recommend is to apply the 3 Stages of Content as taught in the beginning of this book.

As I've mentioned before, creating great content requires the testing of many pieces, and seeing what gets liked by your ideal audience.

Stage 1 is the testing phase -- casual, exploratory, prolific content -- you don't have to spend much effort distributing your Stage 1 content. Just share it with your audience in a simple way such as a Facebook Profile post, or a very small Facebook Post Boost.

However, when your content gets into Stage 2 -- editing and repurposing what's been loved by your ideal audience -- then it makes sense to spend more effort distributing it, re-sharing it.

Finally, when you get to your Stage 3 content, it deserves a lot more effort making sure your audience has seen it multiple times. And, very importantly, sharing it well beyond your audience, too.

You may have heard it said that "Content is King." If that's the case, then Distribution is Queen.

In this chapter, I'll give you several ways to distribute your content.

Where does your ideal audience consume content?

First, let's get clear on this important point:

It's not about sharing your content *everywhere*.

It's about sharing it everywhere *your ideal audience hangs out*.

Therefore, we first need to understand where your ideal audience typically consume your type of content.

For example, if I'm looking to distribute a text-heavy blog post, I'm not going to think about Instagram where people expect images with a fairly concise caption. They're not looking to read epic blog posts.

Or, if I'm writing about spirituality as my side interest, posting it on LinkedIn (a professional platform) isn't the best fit, unless my sole content is about spirituality.

What I will want to do first is to ask my audience (starting with my ideal clients) where they enjoy receiving content like mine.

If it's been awhile since you have asked your clients, it's time to do it. If you don't have clients yet, ask friends who are similar to your ideal client.

Sample Email to Your Clients/Friends

Send an email to 10 clients/friends and give them a few options, plus an open-ended question.

(For greater courtesy & higher response, send out each email individually, not as a CC or BCC to everyone.)

Example:

Hi [Name],

I'm working on creating some helpful content to share my expertise & experience to [name the benefit of your content, e.g. "guide people on reaching their career purpose."]

My questions is: Where should I be sharing the content? I'm curious where and how do you consume content? I'd love to reach more people like you! :)

Which of the following platforms do you enjoy visiting? Where would you expect to see my writings or videos?

[Option 1]

[Option 2]

[Option 3]

[Option 4]

[Option 5]

I'd love to see your top choices.

Or if there's another platform or way of sharing my content, that you would recommend for me, I'd love to know!

Thanks so much for your help!

[Your Name]

PS. Of course, what you share with me will be kept confidential.

If you're sending this out to less than 25 people, there's no need for any software.

Asking your most ideal clients is better than asking a large sample of people who might or might not be ideal clients. You want actionable data. Plus, people are more likely to respond to a personal, email message, instead of an impersonal survey link.

Which options should you ask about?

Before I give you my suggestions, it would be good for you to take a pause and brainstorm how *you* think your ideal clients consume content… I don't want to bias you with my ideas.

Go and do that brainstorming now, before moving on.

Ready?

Here is a comprehensive list of options… choose your 5 favorite options to offer:

- Email Newsletter
- Podcast (if you publish audio content)
- Medium.com (if you write long-form blog posts)
- Facebook

- LinkedIn
- Twitter
- Instagram (if you like sharing images)
- Pinterest
- Snapchat (especially for reaching millennials & younger)
- Google+
- Youtube (if you like sharing videos)
- Blogs (which ones? ask your people)
- Online groups (which ones? ask them)
- Magazines (which ones?)

To prevent overwhelm, just offer a few choices -- your own favorites.

Once you send your email, and you don't hear back in 3 - 5 days, send a follow-up to make sure they got your email. Say that you'd love their response!

You may be surprised by the results of your survey.

Or, it might confirm what you were expecting.

Either way, let those results guide where you share your content going forward!

A simple, effective platform: Your email newsletter

Imagine having 100 people who regularly think about your services. They might refer new clients to you, or become a client themselves.

Now, imagine having to individually email those 100 people every month to keep in touch. That would be way more work than necessary.

There's a better way -- keep in touch via a monthly email newsletter.

You may have more or less than 100 email subscribers... but the point is that it's efficient and effective to keep in touch with a regular rhythm of a newsletter.

After doing marketing full-time since 2009, and personally coaching almost 1,000 business owners, I have seen that among the most important assets for a business is its email subscriber list.

More accurately, the important thing is the *relationship* the business has with its email subscribers. Are they opening the newsletters? Are they clicking through?

First you need to get permission to add people to your email list:

- Be sure that your website has an easy way for people to opt-in to your email newsletter.

- Then you can individually email your clients, past clients, friends and colleagues (who are supportive of your business) and let them know that you are starting your email newsletter, and what topics they can expect to see inside. Give them the link to join your newsletter if they would be interested to read it. Don't pressure them, because you want subscribers who actually will open & click your emails at least occasionally. If almost none of your subscribers are opening & clicking your emails, your newsletter's "email deliverability" goes down, and it starts being relegated to people's "spam" boxes.

To create an email newsletter, I highly recommend Mailchimp -- this is the service I've used since 2009.

To send email newsletters legally (and with the courtesy of easy unsubscribe), you *must* use email marketing services like Mailchimp. Please do *not* use your own email and BCC people. That makes unsubscribing (should they need to) difficult, and it's illegal too.

Once you've created an easy way on your website for people to join your email newsletter, now you can aim to send something simple to your subscribers at least once a month.

A good email newsletter might include one or more of these:

1. **Something Useful** -- a tool, a tip, some piece of advice you think will help your audience, perhaps an "aha!" moment from a recent client session that they can benefit from.

2. **Something Encouraging** -- an inspirational quote or idea.

3. **Something Entertaining** -- something you've come across on the internet that made you laugh or touched you, that would be appropriate to share with your audience too; ideally, that piece of content can be related back to your expertise.

4. **Something Inviting** -- include a low-cost offering (book, workshop, online course), or if it's a higher-end offering, invite them to a complimentary 1-1 consult with you.

You can see all of my recent email newsletters, month by month, here: www.GeorgeKao.com/monthly

Regarding graphics in an email newsletter: it's nice, but not necessary. You can feel free to keep it simple for now! Your readers just want a momentary, inspirational respite, or a simple useful tool. You don't need to send long newsletters like I do. You may eventually add more over time, but don't overwhelm yourself at the beginning before you have a solid rhythm of sending newsletters. Start simple and short!

Start once a month. Then, you may want to eventually build up to once a week.

To show some examples of simple, effective email newsletters, I made this video:
www.FB.com/GeorgeKaoCommunity/videos/10154677773574867

Links mentioned in the video above:

- My own archive of monthly newsletters:
  www.GeorgeKao.com/monthly

- Mailchimp's research on average open & click rates: www.mailchimp.com/resources/research/email-marketing-benchmarks
- My other short video walking through Fiona Moore's email newsletter: www.FB.com/GeorgeKaoCommunity/videos/10153886393729867
- See a screenshot of Sheeba Varghese's simple and effective newsletter:

COACH
Sheeba Varghese
INSPIRING YOU TO THRIVE

Dear GK,

Leadership requires choice and intentionality. It's not just for the executives of the world, but for anyone who takes responsibility for those they influence or are entrusted to their care.

You can *choose* to lead, but examining *how well* you lead is vital to your growth and to those around you. Read more here.

Leadership as a choice

Be Inspired To Thrive,

Thrive In Your Time

Work-Life Balance. It's what we all wish to achieve, but many feel overwhelmed and wonder if it is even possible. In this self-guided coaching program, you will see that balance is possible with a simple but powerful strategy. THRIVE in your time by giving your life balance the attention it needs today!

Click here to learn more.

Notice how concise this email newsletter is -- a simple tip, with a link to read more. She also includes a simple invitation at the bottom of the email to her self-guided coaching program.

Look at the best practices of the platforms you use

Besides an email newsletter (which is important), it's also important to be sharing on larger platforms such as Facebook.

Again, go back to the research I suggested earlier: which platform(s) do your ideal clients love? Besides an email newsletter, **starting with just 1 platform** (such as Facebook) is totally fine.

Once you get the hang of it, you can consider adding another platform.

Whichever one you decide, learn a bit about the best practices and possibilities of that platform:

Step 1. Look at what is being shared on that platform.

> Pay special attention to what is being shared by *your* ideal audience members.
>
> Go to your clients' profile there -- what type of content (from other people) are they sharing? This signals to you what's important to them. Consider creating more content like that.

Step 2. Experiment.

> For example, share the same message 3 different ways (as a text-only status update, as an image, and as a video), and see what your audience likes the most. Especially your *ideal* audience: which posts are they liking the most?

An example of a test: On Facebook, when you are sharing an image quote, it tends to get more views if you *also* include the text of the quote above the image. To see how I discovered this, watch this video: www.FB.com/GeorgeKaoCommunity/videos/10155132082344867

Another Facebook test I did recently showed that my audience prefers my Facebook posts in this order...

1. Directly-uploaded Video (not sharing a Youtube link) = 26 likes, 2 shares
2. Status Update = 22 likes, 2 shares
3. Photo = 14 likes, 4 shares
4. Link = 9 likes, 2 shares

Yet, another client who tested their audience showed that Link Shares got more likes from their audience, than Status Updates or Photos.

The bottom line is that *you need to test your own audience & content* to see what is the most effective distribution method for your audience.

The Best Distribution is Guesting

Typically you will be sharing content with your own audience, through your email newsletter and on your social media.

However, to reach far more people in an efficient manner, it's all about guesting, which includes:

- Guest blogging -- writing an article for someone else's blog
- Guest speaking -- speaking to someone else's audience / at their event
- Teleclass or Webinar for someone else's audience

When you guest, your content is endorsed by that influencer to their audience. You have credibility with the audience right away.

There are 4 reasons why influencers might want to share your content...

Reason 1. When their audience needs your help...

This is when an influencer is getting questions from their audience, but that influencer is not herself an expert in that area.

Can the influencer clearly see that your expertise would be a great complement to what they are teaching?

How would you know? Sometimes you'll see comments on that influencer's blog, or on their social media, which are questions that you would love to answer.

Another way is to simply guess: does that influencer talk about things that are related (but not competitive) to what you specialize in?

You might be a blessing for them, if you came along and did a free webinar for their audience, or if you wrote a guest blog for them.

Another possibility is for you to *substitute* for them in a way that would give them more time. For example, I substituted on a coaching call for a colleague, and although I sold nothing on the call, I got a new client from that 1 hour group call.

The point is to frame it in your mind (and in theirs) as a service to them:

You are providing a relief for that influencer, that they now have a trusted resource (you) to refer their people to.

In the early years of my business, I approached people who had audiences that wanted to learn Social Media. (That used to be my primary area of expertise.) I made sure the Influencer herself didn't teach it, so that I wasn't a competitor, but a collaborator.

I had several partners who promoted me to their audience of thousands, and each one promoted me several times in those first few years, *because I had expertise their audience urgently wanted.*

When it works well, it is a true win-win-win:

- The audience get answers they've been looking for.
- The influencer builds goodwill with their audience (and earns commissions, if appropriate, from helping you sell your services.)
- You get an additional audience to serve.

Reason 2. When an influencer frequently publishes quality content.

Sometimes you'll come across a platform (blog, website, podcast, or social media page) that shares quality content very frequently, e.g. daily blog posts.

If you notice that the content isn't always written by the owner of that platform, then there might be an opportunity for you to become a contributor.

Examples of popular (large) platforms that welcome guest writing:

- HuffingtonPost.com
- ThriveGlobal.com
- ElephantJournal.com
- GoodMenProject.com
- Curejoy.com
- HeySigmund.com
- Entrepreneur.com
- Forbes.com
- FinerMinds.com
- EvolveAndAscend.com
- Collective-Evolution.com
- MindBodyGreen.com

- (Know of another large platform that welcomes guesting? Let me know.)

In fact, any popular blog in your industry (or in a related industry) could fit the bill. Take a few minutes to brainstorm! You'll then start seeing more of them naturally. We tend to find what we're actively looking for!

The reason why such platforms allow guest postings -- as long as it fits their quality standards -- is due to their business model. They earn money primarily from advertisements on their website. They want to keep visitors coming back frequently to see quality content.

So look for the platforms/channels that frequently have content that's not of their own making. If your content is relevant there, it could be a blessing if you offered high quality *free* content for them.

Note: Bigger platforms sometimes require exclusive content, or at least that the content you post there be exclusive to their platform for 3-6 months, then you are allowed to post it on your own blog too. I think it's worth it, if it gets you more website visitors than your own blog post would.

Reason 3. An influencer is intrigued by your content

Sometimes, you'll meet an influencer who is intrigued by what you do. Maybe you're able to personally help them.

Their audience might not even have asked for it, but if the influencer truly believes it would be beneficial for their audience, they might bring you on to do a guest thing.

In exchange for promoting you to their audience, you could give the influencer some of your private 1-1 time (coaching, counseling, consulting), or you could offer that influencer special access to your product/service.

Reason 4. You can co-create content with an influencer.

Perhaps you know an influencer (or simply: a friend/colleague with an audience) and you could imagine creating some content together? For example, a conversation on a topic of interest to both of you, where you each could bring your own perspective?

I usually do a co-creative conversations with a colleague about once a month. Often, both of us share it, and we are each discovered by new audience members.

Make "guesting" one of your key marketing activities

Guesting helps you reach many more people. When you guest, you have instant credibility with a new group of people.

It will also stretch your content creation abilities, since your partner may give you some feedback to improve your content (they want great quality for their audience!)

So resolve today to put Guesting as an important aim in your regular marketing habits.

Even if you are just starting out, and the idea of guesting seems overwhelming, I encourage you to start small, if only to look for and begin building relationships with service providers with whom you feel a natural synergy, for future potential collaboration.

Where to look for guest content opportunities?

Start with the people you know.

Look at your contacts list, and reach out to people who are supportive of you. Some may be influencers, or some may be able to connect you with someone who is.

Be sure to think about the 4 reasons listed above, and in your message to them, express how your collaboration would specifically benefit them and their audience.

As you gain experience, you can branch out to people you don't know yet (think of them as potential new friends.) Observe where your ideal audience is already gathered, where your topic is already relevant.

Some ideas of what to look for…

- Websites that have a prominent email opt-in (newsletter)
- Blogs in your field
- Blogs in related fields
- Medium.com publications (search a relevant keyword there)
- Facebook groups
- LinkedIn groups
- Online forums
- Youtube (search for channels with interviews, where each interview there received at least 100 views.)
- Podcasters (ideally as a guest post or live webinar for their audience)
- Popular Facebook pages (you could pay the influencer to boost your post)
- Popular Twitter users
- Printed magazines
- Organizations, Companies, Associations
- Google Search: [Related Topic that interests your audience] AND newsletter
- Authors (search on Amazon) of related topics -- see if they have a blog or newsletter
- Where your niche mates are being interviewed (google it)
- Where your niche mates are guest blogging
- Clients of yours who have an audience
- Ideal clients' social media profiles: If they're sharing someone else's articles, videos, links, then those sources may be influencers you want to reach out to.

Again, in your outreach, remember the 4 reasons why influencers might share your content, and be smart about which reason(s) you express to the influencer.

Approach an influencer with a balance of **confidence** (if you truly believe you can help their audience) and **humility** (don't assume they should say yes... be gentle, and let them decide.)

If it is a good match, you won't need to cajole them into it. They will want it.

Chapter 14: Keeping Track of Your Best Content

Over time, you'll wish that you have some way to track the best content you've posted: which of your pieces have done well, and to remind you which topics you've been neglecting to share.

There are different ways this could be done well. You could use document, or a mindmap, or a spreadsheet, for example. The key is to find what works for you and do it consistently, so that you gather in one place an analysis of what content is working well. to help guide your ongoing content creation.

Personally, I use and recommend Google Spreadsheets. I love that it is free, and relatively easy to use. Here are some of the things I track that may also be helpful to you:

- *Date last shared*
    - Simply the date you shared that piece.
    - When it is a meaningful or popular piece of content, share it every few months. Once you do, update this date with the date you last shared it.

- *Overall Idea / Keywords*
    - Here's where you concisely/briefly describe the piece of content. You might include some keywords so it's easy for you to search the spreadsheet and find that content again later.

- *Link*
    - What's the link to that piece of content?
    - On Facebook, Twitter, Google+, you can get the specific link or URL for any piece of content by clicking the timestamp of that piece.

- *Topic*
    - Over time you'll come to some kind of standardized way to describe what topics you generally create content on.

- *Where you shared it*
    - Whichever platforms you've decided on, such as Facebook, LinkedIn, Twitter, as well as Your Blog, Your Email Newsletter.

- *Optional Columns:*
    - Importance of that piece of content to you (no matter how popular it is)
    - Frequency (how often -- in months -- you would like to reshare that content, e.g. 6 = 6 months, 0.5 = every 2 weeks.)
    - Next -- this is the date that you would like to re-share that piece of content.

NOTE: don't worry about making the perfect system. It is more important that you are tracking your content, and that you are using it to remind you of what topics to share next.

Chapter 15: Create a rhythm of content sharing that works for you

The most successful content creators usually seem to have a rhythm or schedule for creating & sharing content.

One hero in the content world is Seth Godin, who has consistently blogged every day for years. If you look at his amazing archive of posts, it took 2 years of consistent blogging *before* his posts began to find *a few people* willing to share them.

It wasn't until about *his 8th year* of consistent blogging, that his blog posts starting getting popular! Today, he is known as one of the top leaders for how to do marketing and leadership in a generous way.

(By the way, it doesn't have to take you 8 years. Perhaps it'll take you only 8 months or 8 weeks to start getting traction... shorten the time by diligently applying the advice in this book!)

How might you have that kind of staying power? Keep reminding yourself of the purposes of your content. That's why I devoted a whole chapter to it at the beginning. Review it again if you need to!

Practice a consistent rhythm of content creation.

"Habits are cobwebs at first, cables at last." (Chinese proverb)

My weekly content rhythm goes like this:

- Saturday: on my long dog walk, I record 3 casual, Stage 1 videos. When I get home, I upload it to Youtube and Facebook, but I don't publish it yet.

- Monday, Wednesday, Friday at 8:30am -- each of these days, I write the article to one of the videos and publish it on:

- My Facebook Biz Page: www.FB.com/GeorgeKaoCommunity
- My LinkedIn: www.linkedin.com/in/GeorgeKao
- My Google Plus: www.google.com/+GeorgeKaoCommunity
- My Twitter: www.twitter.com/GeorgeKao
- I also post the video/article of the previous day to my Facebook Profile: www.FB.com/GeorgeKao

- Tuesday afternoon: I schedule my Email Newsletter to be sent on Wednesday morning. You can subscribe to it here: www.GeorgeKao.com/newsletter

It took me months of experimenting with different schedules, before I settled on this rhythm.

Allow your rhythms to change over time. For 2015, my rhythm was to make a new video every weekday. Once I got to video #100, I scaled back to doing 3 videos a week.

So what about you?

What rhythm will you experiment with now?

Stick with your rhythm, until you feel the need to tweak it. Once you tweak it, stick with that new rhythm for awhile.

Keep coming back to the purpose of your content so you can stay inspired... until your content rhythm becomes a habit!

Chapter 16: Even when conditions are not good, I still do my content...

Sometimes, you may really need a break (like when you are very ill), but other times, we can let minor circumstances, like being a little tired or feeling like we'd rather watch a TV show, get in the way of keeping our commitments to ourselves (and to our audience.)

It is truly an art to know the difference, and only you know for sure whether you genuinely need a break, or if you're slacking off.

Do your best to push through when you might be otherwise be tempted to slack, and do you best to honor your need for self care when that is genuinely called for.

Example:

I wasn't feeling up for making this video...
www.FB.com/GeorgeKao/posts/10106312959225913

Conditions were sub-optimal -- I was dealing with seasonal allergies; I forgot my selfie stick so I had to hold the camera with my arm stretched out; I was at a park I rarely go to, so my dog wasn't familiar with the place; and to top it off, I wasn't sure what I was going to say in the video.

Yet, because I have a rhythm of content creation that I'm dedicated to following, I made the video anyway.

Whereas I've become accustomed to usually doing my videos in 1-3 takes, this time due to sub-optimal conditions, it took me 5 takes... but it ended up ok.

It always will turn out fine. Give into your higher impulse (sometimes it's very quiet, a tiny impulse) in the moment to move yourself -- literally, it often requires moving your body off of the floor -- out of your slump, and do something useful. Every time you do this, you will feel a sense of accomplishment, and be just a bit stronger the next time you're in a slump.

If you always wait until you feel good and ready, and conditions are optimal, before doing your work, you will rarely do it. You will find yourself taking way too long to build your content. Remember: great content comes from publishing often, to see what works, and therefore what to improve on and re-distribute.

Your impetus for action must come from within, rather than depending on external factors, if you want to become a prolific content creator in your field, if you want to break through writer's block, if you want to free yourself up to give your gifts.

Free yourself from the pressure to be perfect, and simply take action.

And that imperfect action, taken over and over again, creates a momentum that sustains itself over time.

Yes, it is normal to occasionally slip, but as with most things, the sooner you get back at it, the better.

This is how we humans act when we are unconscious:

Feel Good ➜ Do Right

(We only do the right thing when we feel good, or conditions are perfect.)

Instead, flip it around and realize that if you act rightly, you end up feeling good. This is exercising your free will, practicing an "internal locus of motivation", thus becoming stronger in your abilities to do the right thing.

Do Right ➜ Feel Good

So, instead of "Do whatever feels good in the moment" I encourage you to "Do the right thing in every moment."

It is a practice -- don't be perfectionistic about it. Just keep coming back to this idea and trying it again, and again, and again. You will become more capable over time!

Here's a nuance that can help:

(Think Good) →(Feel a little better) →Do Right →Feel Good

Whenever it feels particularly challenging to do the right thing (i.e. when conditions are poor for doing your work), try to *use your mind & heart for a minute* to feel a little bit better... then, move into doing the right thing.

Think about the LANGUAGE you tell yourself. Just a few thoughts to try on:

- *I appreciate the chance I get to do this*
- *I am so grateful for the opportunity to share my message*
- *Any content I create, even casually, is better than nothing*

Also, you might try to see IMAGES in your mind about that activity: visualize yourself enjoying the work or doing it gracefully.

Use your mind and heart! Once you feel a little bit better, move into doing the right thing, right away. Do not hesitate. **The true feel-good comes *after* doing the right thing.**

A little framework that might be helpful for you:

Plan:
- Visualize what is the right thing
- Make it a stretch, but don't overstretch yourself
- Have a rhythm for your work that is productive, yet doable

Practice:
- When you're procrastinating, use your mind & heart, for a minute, to reconnect to your sense of Purpose and Love
- Process over Product: the process you are practicing is the most important thing -- let the result turn out however it does
- You'll never act perfectly (nor will conditions ever be). Perfection is actually in the whole picture of your life... it has a perfect beauty to it.
- My example: I have never made a "perfect" video... I just keep releasing them, and improving over time.

Praise:
- Praise yourself, or God (if you believe), for helping you to do the right thing.
- This builds more trust in that source of power for the next time you're called to do the right thing.

This practice of DO RIGHT →FEEL GOOD, will allow you to excel in your work, and in your personal life, and become more successful than most.

To watch the accompanying video and comment on this chapter, go here:
www.FB.com/GeorgeKao/posts/10106312959225913

Need more motivational methods to get into your content rhythm?

Read about the 8 motivational methods:
www.FB.com/GeorgeKaoCommunity/posts/10154820175689867

Chapter 17: Share from your heart -- and trust the process!

When it comes to content creation, here is a harsh truth... but at the same time, strangely wonderful:

No one is going to remember any of your content, except the few pieces that are *really* good.

So don't worry about making content that isn't good.

Let's look at the example of musicians. They are known for their most popular songs. Their unpopular or "bad" songs? No one remembers those, except for their hard core fans.

Authors are remembered for their award-winning novels, but few remember their mediocre writings.

This principle holds true on social media as well. Facebook's algorithm only features the popular stuff in the news feed. They rarely display the posts that got few or no likes.

Same thing when it comes to search engines: If people love a webpage, they will link to it, and Google will bump it up in the search rankings. If no one is linking to a bad webpage, it goes into obscurity.

Here's what this means for you: **You can feel liberated to create and share.**

Share more of your thoughts. Write more about your framework. Talk about the "aha!" moments in your work with clients. Post occasional invitations to work with your business. If it's good, it will spread.

Always remember: what's "good" content is not up to you to decide.

Your role is to create and share. It's your *audience's role* to decide whether that content is worth remembering.

If it is worth it, they will let you know by their likes, comments, and shares.

If however you don't see much engagement -- (if you get crickets!) -- then it's your audience's gentle feedback that they didn't think much of it. *No matter how important it felt to you.* What you do is simply this: move on to create and share the next thing.

(The other possibility, if you get silence, is that you aren't sharing that piece with the right audience. If you feel that it's an important piece of content, find another audience to share it with.)

Believe me, there have been many things I've shared that I felt were really important... but *you* (my audience) didn't think so. :-)

So there was silence. Nobody is to blame.

It's simply the constant illusion that we content creators experience: the delusion of content grandeur. Just because I created a piece of content, it feels important to me. Think about the origami builders I mentioned earlier in the book.

Same for you: if you spend time recording a video or writing a blog post, it will feel important to you. The more time we invest in something, the more significant it feels to us.

Sometimes, we get lucky and our content is loved by our audience.

(We can dramatically increase our luck by sharing lots of content!)

When that happens, our content will be picked up by the internet and social media, and generously shown to others who weren't part of our audience... new people might then decide to join our tribe.

However, most of the time -- *this is simply statistics* -- much of our content doesn't go viral. It might be barely liked by our audience.

Remember this:

Nobody will remember your *"meh"* pieces of content.

You are therefore liberated to share as much content as you want.

There is an important foundational point:

As long as you ground yourself and your actions in a spirit of service and helping, then you win, and so will your audience.

Whenever you share content, you are learning, simply because you are practicing.

If your audience happens to like it, you win because more people are seeing it.

If no one likes it, you still win because by creating and sharing, you are getting practice with experimenting and expressing your voice and message.

I encourage you to feel great whenever you share something you think is worthwhile... no matter what others think of it.

However; if you do not ground yourself in a spirit of true service and helping, but instead you act from an energetic state of fear or grasping, and you take advantage of people by trying to manipulate them into liking, sharing, or buying, *they will unfortunately remember.*

I made this mistake in the first few years of my business.

I shared content and offers primarily out of a fear that I wouldn't make enough money or get enough popularity, or out of greed (wanting to make even more money or be even more popular)... and in those early years, I ended up taking advantage of people.

Back then, I was freely sharing teaser-only content, but not the real stuff. That good stuff? I made my audience pay for. I pretended to give "free trainings!" but they were a carefully designed sales pitches to get them to buy the real stuff later.

Many of those previous audience members never forgave nor forgot...

Even though I'm in my 8th year of business, it feels like I really only began my business 3 years ago, when I started to share content freely, by practicing the principles in this book. It's like I lost 5 years in my business because I wasn't being mindful about content.

Ever since I shifted my intentions to being of service in my content, I began to build a new audience, one I could really build a relationship with, one who could truly trust me.

It is sometimes painful to think about my past, but I am glad to be practicing a more long-term way of doing business now. I am grateful for the growth I've experienced.

Now, it feels like a blessing to create and generously share, from a spirit of service and helping. It fills everyone's hearts.

To watch a companion video or comment on this chapter: www.FB.com/GeorgeKaoCommunity/videos/10154234909344867

There's another related video I made that you might find helpful canned "Overcoming Fear in Creating Content" -- www.FB.com/GeorgeKaoCommunity/videos/10154897264789867

You are truly special...

Very few people care enough about authentic marketing to pick up this book.

Even fewer people read it to the end!

You are truly special. I'm so grateful for your care and attention.

The problem is: I don't know who you are :)

If you are willing, help me learn a bit about you by going to this short online form to let me know who you are:
www.GeorgeKao.com/BookSurvey

I personally read every response.

Once you fill out the form, you'll also be able to access some bonus content.

Perhaps we will meet someday. I look forward to that possibility!

--George Kao

Can you help by adding a review?

Would you like to help this book get discovered?

Every single review helps new people to find this book. It spreads the message of Authentic Content -- you make a real difference when you write a review.

1. Go to http://www.Amazon.com
2. Search for this book and go to the book's page.

3. Click on "Write a review". It doesn't have to be long. Consider briefly answering these questions:

- What type of person would you recommend this book to?
- What did you most love learning from the book?
- Is there another book or resource that you recommend, in conjunction with this one? People are more likely then to mark your review as "helpful"

Thank you, from the bottom of my heart.

George Kao
www.GeorgeKao.com

Acknowledgements

This book is the result of many people's support.

First, I thank my wife for her love and encouragement. Without her support, I might never have written this book.

Secondly, my email subscribers and social media audience -- those who watch my videos and comment on my posts -- without you, I would not know which pieces of my content was good enough to include in this book! Thank you for your continued loving attention and encouragement. Truly, I write for you.

To my individual Clients and the MasterHeart group -- my deep gratitude to you for supporting my livelihood. I am so fortunate to have the opportunity to serve you. It is a joy to watch your growth, learning, and connections, as you build your authentic business.

To my "advisory circle" which I gathered to edit this book and give suggestions on many things including the Title -- I consider you the co-creators of this book. Special thanks to Christine for coming up with the idea for the book cover image!

To Paul Zelizer who wrote the Foreword to this book -- thank you for your trust in me! I am truly honored by your willingness to support this book. Dear Reader, check out Paul's links: www.Awarepreneurs.com and www.PaulZelizer.com

To those who wrote an advance review/blurb for this book -- thank you for your generosity and trust. You have given me energy and courage to keep doing even better work, so that we might together co-create a world with more compassion, authenticity, and wisdom. Dear Reader, here are their links. I encourage you to support these authentic businesses:

Terra Christoff, Ph.D., Soul Purpose Coach for Women
www.TerraChristoff.com

Joe Pulizzi, Founder of Content Marketing Institute
www.JoePulizzi.com

Katharina Zuleger, Visionary & Mentor
www.Aquarian-Leaders.com

Jason Stein, Business Coach for Wellness Providers
www.JasonStein.com

Fiona Moore, Transformative Mentor and Healer
www.FionaMoore.com

David B. Younger, Ph.D, Clinical Psychologist and creator of Love After Kids
www.LoveAfterKids.com

Alisoun Mackenzie, The Compassionate Business Mentor, Speaker and Author
www.alisoun.com

Stephen Dynako, Author of "The Self Aware Lover"
www.dynako.com

Claire Shamilla, Energy Healer
www.ClaireShamilla.com

Alison Weeks, Business Coach and Lifelong Educator
(link not available at this time)

Andy Burton, Author, Speaker & Dream Goal Coach
www.EagerlyGrowing.com

Cindy Belz, Founder of Footsteps of Wisdom
www.FootstepsOfWisdom.com

Denise Adele Trudeau Poskas, PhD, Leadership & Human Strategist Coach www.BlueEggLeadership.com

Keith Logan, Sustainable Community Development Consultant
https://www.linkedin.com/in/keith-logan-186b46a/

Anastasia Netri, Core Genius Coaching
www.anastasianetri.com

Lauchlan Mackinnon
www.lauchlanmackinnon.com

Liesel Teversham, Confidence and Strengths Coach for Introverts
www.savvyselfgrowth.com

Maia Duerr, organizational consultant, coach, author of *Work That Matters*
www.MaiaDuerr.com

Tad Hargrave, Founder of www.MarketingforHippies.com

About The Author

Since 2009, George Kao has been a trusted conscious marketing mentor to thousands of coaches, counselors, consultants, speakers, and authors.

His mission is to raise the marketing effectiveness of those who prioritize integrity, compassion, and generosity in their business.

George's specialty is helping people grow their ideal audience through authentic online marketing, including social media, content marketing, webinars / online workshops, authentic networking, mindful joint-ventures (JV's), launch planning, and business productivity & simplicity. George has done thousands of 1-1 business coaching sessions with clients.

He has taught tens of thousands of people through webinars, teleclasses, telesummits, and in-person workshops.

For many wisdom-based solopreneurs around the world, George Kao is the go-to expert and advisor re: heart-based marketing, and how to create a business that is truly ethical and fulfilling.

George helps clients stabilize their income, expand their visibility online, and structure their business so that they can experience freedom and joy in their work.

You can access his comprehensive free content through his website, www.GeorgeKao.com